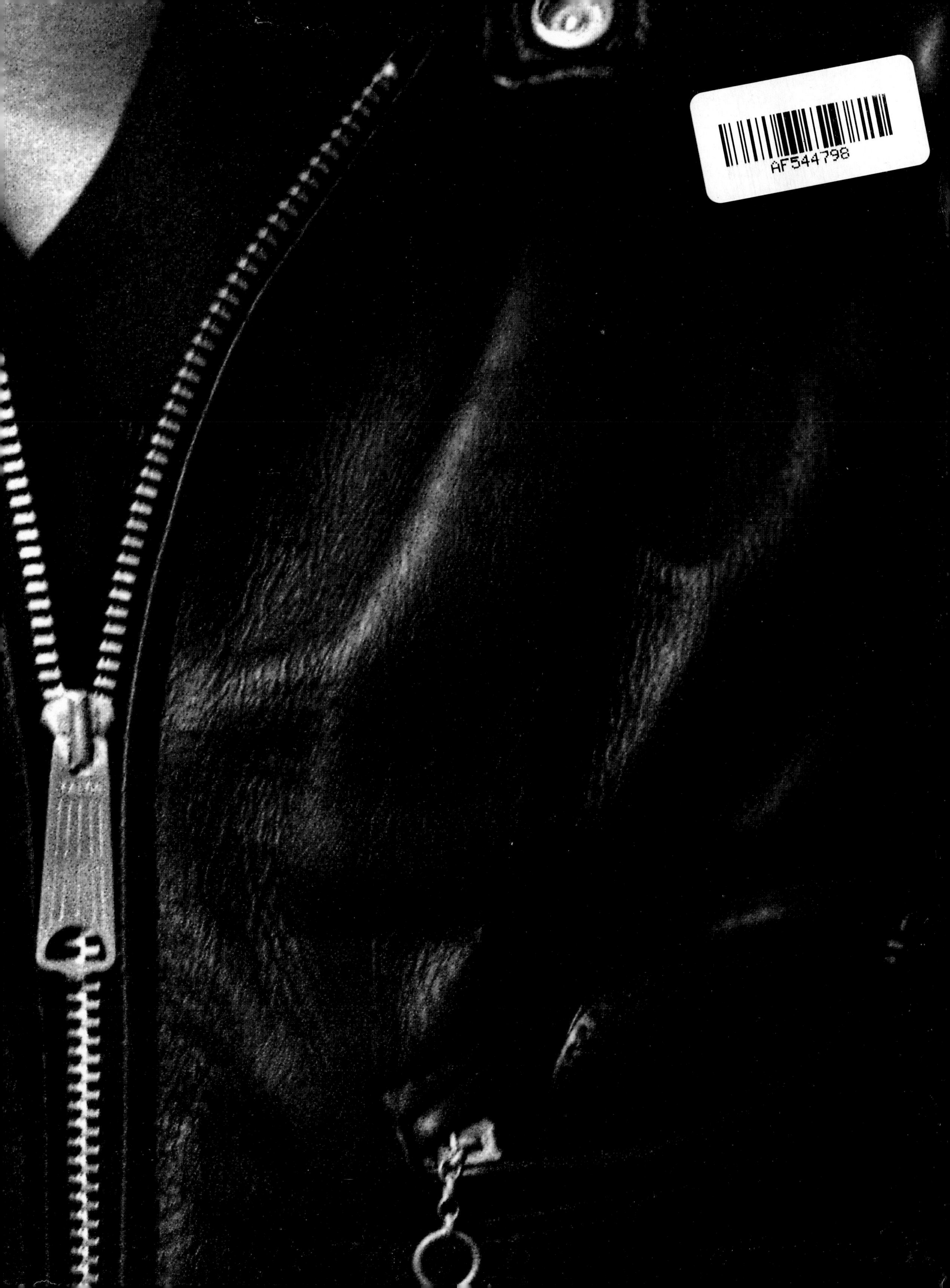

gerard malanga
RESISTANCE TO MEMORY

gerard malanga
RESISTANCE TO MEMORY

poem by

THURSTON MOORE

text by

BEN MADDOW

ARENA EDITIONS

to: from: gerard thurston

A New York boy has awkward grace
—beautiful face
subway, school room
dogs and girls
bless you America for leaving angels
to their own device

intuition is the goddess trait
discover poetry through old grey shapes
Gerard is ready to honor women

"The photographs I was taking of various friends and
acquaintances I thought were important. Not
because I was taking them but because of
the subject matter."

no light meter – free syntax
are you ready for your screen test?
and which side will the stars reside?
Andy and Gerard have created proto-photo:
instill the still image with magic:
show the world its sprocket holes.
Gerard's thing is something else.

it all happened so slow
rock n roll
rolling stones
anita pallenberg glowing in flushed lost
lust – patti smith nailing NYC's heart
to her chest — william burroughs deadpans
a million dreams — angus maclise and
wallace berman, kindred artists of a time
when america needed them most.
remember
remember
remember the poets.
–here are eyes–

Thurston Moore

acts of friendship

We have a great deal more kindness than is ever spoken.

R. W. Emerson, 1841

When I was rather young, and my passion for the photographic image was shared by only a few enthusiasts, I had the curious fantasy that I might live long enough to see every photograph ever made. It seemed to me, and it still does, that even the most routine, unskillful specimen, taken casually or in bad taste or even accidentally, has some corner of great interest—if only that one has never seen it before. And this is the consequence of the miracle itself: that the real world imposes its complex intensity on microscopic grains of metal. If this is true of the dull billions of photographs, how much more true of the craftsman, the photographer whose work one sees for the first time. On opening the sealed boxes, and first viewing the labors of Gerard Malanga, one feels, in spite of one's hard earned skepticism, a sensation of spontaneous pleasure. Each image is an act of friendship, and consciously so. Malanga writes,

Nothing is faked or was done for any other purpose than as archival remembrance. I believe each person, as it were, gave me their picture.

In this respect, as in others, Malanga is not following the fashion current among the ambitious to create a new personal photography by shredding and reassembling the image, or by inventing or rearranging nature for the camera, or by altering it in the primitive chemistry of the darkroom. Such works are not inherently bad; one has the right to use any technical means to produce the art one honestly wants; but dishonesty, as to intention, is all too common, particularly among the untrained talents. It's as if they fear nature, both people and things, as too powerful to be wholly controlled; and of course they are right. It is not a new cowardice as Da Vinci remarked in his treatise on anatomy:

Although human subtlety makes a variety of inventions answering by different means to the same end, it will never devise an invention more beautiful, more simple, or more direct than does nature. . . .

But each artist must make this crucial choice: shall he look outward toward the crowded world or inward to the equally tumultuous self. The first choice is classic, and characterizes the earliest half century of photography; the second choice is romantic, a dramatization of the self. Whereas the first can lead to the boredom, of say, endless banal American landscapes, the second can lead to the irritations of empty self-aggrandizement.

Malanga is never, as Cartier-Bresson was in his earliest work, hostile to his subjects, as that greatest miniaturist since Fouquet, almost declared himself to be:

The mere presence of the photographer and his camera affects the behavior of the "victim."

Malanga's subjects are as kindly as he is kindly. So he is certainly not like Richard Avedon, who for years hated the celebrities who were his assigned subjects; and whose habitual cruelty, as much now of method as of attitude, gave us several years ago his corrosive book of ordinary, Western, small town Americans. Malanga perhaps admires, as most of us do, the work of Diane Arbus, who hid her enjoyment of horror under the pretense of sudden friendship. Living in the same New York world, Malanga is never sinister. It is all a matter of character, after all. Nor is he at all like the camera poetess Helen Levitt, who, except for a lovely, serene New York gypsy series, is a secret hunter, who listens for drama on the stage of the stoop or the sidewalk, pursues it anonymously, seizes it, and disappears. And yet these are all portraitists working in the same venerable genre that began at the beginning, at the first discovery of the magic image.

Malanga has firmly made the classic choice; in his self-portraits, there is not the furious morbidity with which some photographers look at themselves. Nor is he afraid of an amiable if modest self-examination. It's interesting that there is, as far as I know, only one self-portrait in which he stands alone, reflected in an ornate Mid-East mirror, the Nikon held up alongside him as a third eye. One is reminded of Nadar's sidelong self-portrait, or Lewis Carroll's portrait of himself holding a gigantic lens. In his four other self-portraits, Malanga appears with others: a woman wrapped in a coarse hide coat (Plate 71), with his father in Florida, in Charles Henri Ford's Dakota apartment, and behind a group of famous friends—famous not to the public, but to the world village that might be defined as simply the assembly of his acquaintances.

Malanga's open and amiable portraits spring directly from his character as he says:

I don't try and trap my subject off his guard because I don't believe it would reveal something about him if I did so. This leads to tricks in the end. I don't do things that way. I can't. I don't have that kind of intelligence. I don't want to give the medium of photography more of a bad reputation than it already has. On the contrary, I want my subject to be as fully aware. . .

He has been gently accused of making ordinary people famous and famous people ordinary; there is some truth to this observation: Malanga likes sociological games and easily casts the meticulous William Burroughs as an ad for summer wear (Plate 16), Tennessee Williams as the friendly neighbor (Plate 26), Kenneth Rexroth as a novelty buttons manufacturer, forever on the verge of bankruptcy, Lawrence Durrell as a fax repairman (Plate 67), Christopher Isherwood as a CPA (Plate 27), Roman Polanski as a pool shark (Plate 31), Lotte Lenya as a little lady who loves her cat (Plate 33), and Jorge Luis Borges as an amiable fortune teller (Plate 45). And he's made portraits of unknown persons—unknown to me at least—who look like seers and tzadikim: the secret ones who save mankind from its perennial follies. And then there are those personalities who cannot resist a bit of self-satire: Abbie Hoffman as a pre-Duncan dancer (Plate 14); Allen Ginsberg, with skull and beads, performing a mysterious mudhra (Plate 1); Robert Mapplethorpe as a charming teenager who's just swiped a few items from the local costume jewelry counter (Plate 22); John Cage conducting an imaginary silence (Plate 42); Zero Mostel pouting like a rhinoceros (Plate 38); and, in a self-parody, Andy Warhol pretending to feel up the esoteric cineaste Parker Tyler.

These intellectual amusements are possible because Malanga gives us the unadulterated person, defensive pretense and all—this is his talent. There is nothing here of the varnished celebrities of

Karsh. Malanga is straight on, like Nadar or the great Carjat. This is possible for him, because like Nadar, Malanga is friend to and admirer of his subjects. He is one of a subgroup of people, difficult to define, who mostly know and interact with one another. It is a circle of individuals by no means confined to Warhol's Factory, for whom Malanga worked as an artisan, writer, and editor, and which was by its nature a very loose confederation of talents. It is a culture defined less by belief and somewhat more by its daily habits: of sleeping and waking and working and partying, by its inheritance of Zen and other Buddhist ideas left from the explorations of the Beats. This group is most clearly defined by its saints: Jack Kerouac, William Burroughs, Marcel Duchamp, Mick Jagger, and Allen Ginsberg, and by the benevolently nihilist values by which they judged Western society. With all this, there is in most of them, and in Malanga too, a brave innocence. The brush and the burin have a certain will of their own; but the camera, that supremely pliable instrument, more than graphics, more than poetry, is the ideal machine for this not quite definable circus of artists. Very much like any extended family, they loved to take pictures of one another.

When Jay McInerny visits Mick Jagger for *Esquire* he describes the apartment in New York:

There are a few knickknacks on the mantle, a button that reads R&R

Nigger, and an eyedrop bottle of jasmine-burning incense. A huge portrait of Gerard Malanga, poet and Warhol friend, also leans on the mantle, awaiting a more permanent mooring.

Photographs are thus, among many other things, a form of social bonding, and they imply the great importance of human personality. Here are Malanga's remarks on the poet Ira Cohen:

To be in Ira's presence is to experience him from beginning to end, so much so that to encounter him unexpectedly halfway around the world one rainy afternoon at my favorite Tibetan luncheonette in Upper Dharmsala, in northern India, is to be at home with him everywhere.

Or this, on John Rechy, in Venice, California:

When visiting with John in L.A. I would sleep on the couch. One morning as John passed from the living room to the kitchen he stopped in front of his mother's picture and holding it up kissed it and returned it to the desk. He was unaware of my being witness.

The purpose of these observations, as well as of the photographs, is to make a library of personality that grows richer with time. Malanga elaborates:

I discovered images I would not have seriously considered at the time of having made them. But I truly believe photographs have this innate and unique ability to take on new significance with age.

Malanga is the photo-historian of this culture; and, by self-definition, a voyeur though I wonder if he's right. A true monomaniacal voyeur has, metaphysically anyway, lined up his penis with the metal keyhole; the view is limited. Malanga has quite a different outlook: he has a broad, clear-headed, amoral stance; he is truly an archivist, motivated by an inherent curiosity about the world and a desire to look and make a record of that looking.

In this attitude, one can see the influence of Warhol's love for reality. In fact, even *Flesh*, *Trash*, and *Heat*, the astonishing Paul Morrissey films that came from the Warhol group, were archival of human events. They were dreams that drew from the spectator neither tears nor tremors. Like Malanga's portraits, they were almost Brechtian observations; what Malanga has added is the warmth, the sympathy of his own character.

Malanga has that great essential virtue of the photographer: humility before the complex splendor of the real thing. The portraits he's made resemble the extraordinary pictures in marble of humans left to us by early Roman sculptors, who showed particular persons exactly as seen.

This is a classical time for self-assessment. In what direction does one hope he will go? Ought he to extend his personal vision, at once sympathetic and truthful, to portraits far outside his own group? People might be indifferent, or even loathe to cooperate in the sort of portraits he's been doing for twenty years. In short, ought Malanga to pursue the faces of strangers? There is both opportunity and danger in such a move. Can Malanga become one of those rare artists who, in Cartier-Bresson's formula, "bare witness to our epoch?" Meantime, we have this wonderful collection to enjoy—and joy is the color of his work.

Ought he go further into the darker regions of the human animal, into the circles of madness, grief, and stupidity, or is he to explore the higher, the more ardent air of wisdom and ironic serenity? Ought one to obey the Platonic imperative, as Emerson contends:

In a portrait [the artist] must inscribe the character and not the features, and must esteem the man who sits to him as himself only an imperfect picture or likeness of the aspiring original within.

One cannot will such an achievement. Even Cartier-Bresson reached this kind of insight only occasionally, in his portraits of Sartre on a bridge; of Matisse among his doves; of old, mad Pound; or Etienne Carjat in his portrait of Baudelaire; or Helen Levitt's keen and loving observation of James Agee. Such portraits are beyond the mere exercise of the will; they approach Emerson's dictum,

The work of art is then beautiful when it begins to be incomprehensible. . .

Malanga's work is not incomprehensible in this transcendental sense, and for this kindly phase of his development, it need not be. There are riches enough here for everyone. Each portrait comments upon and supports the others, forming a broad collective portrait of his friends and their wild and gentle prophets.

Ben Maddow

plates

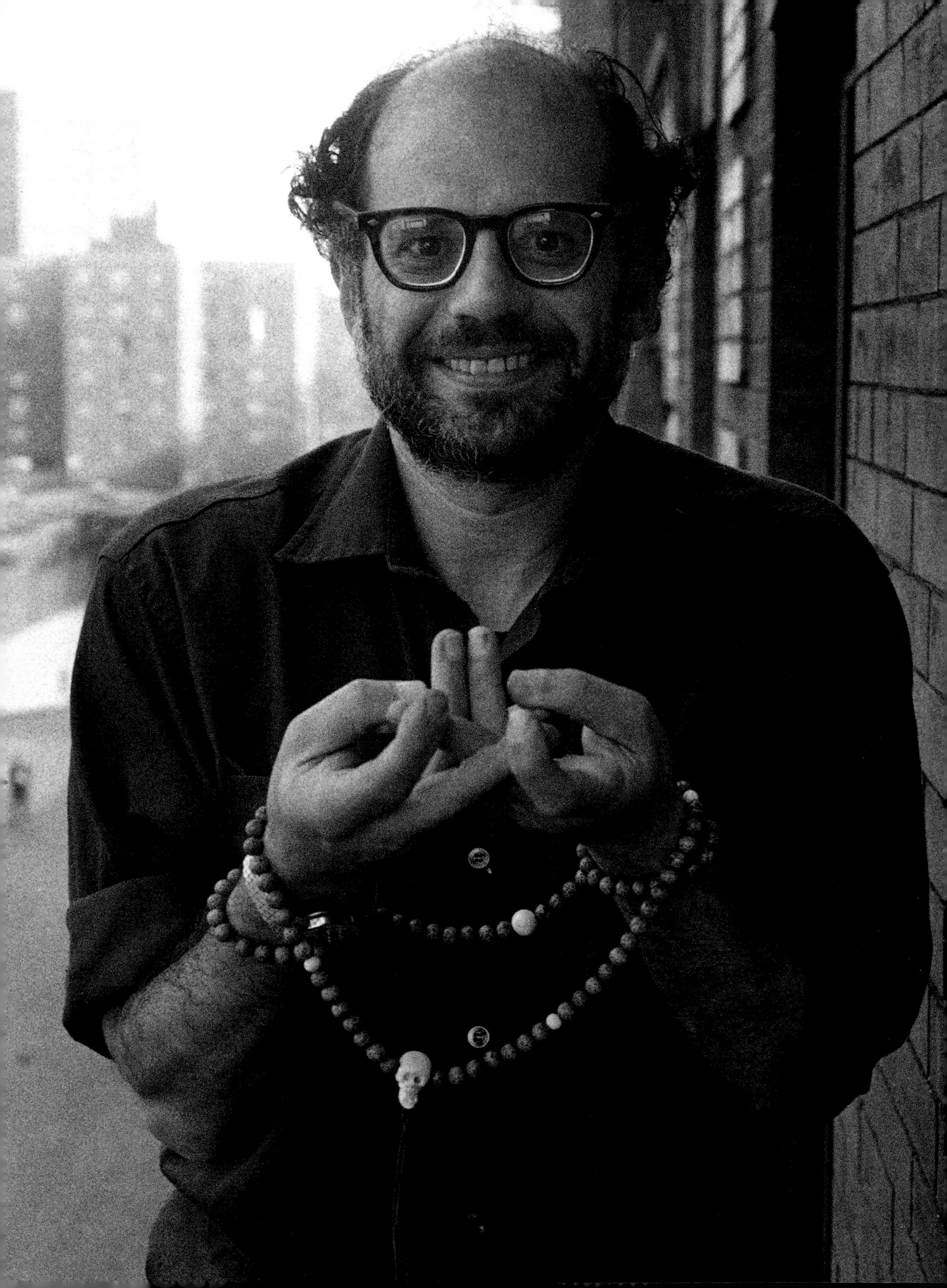

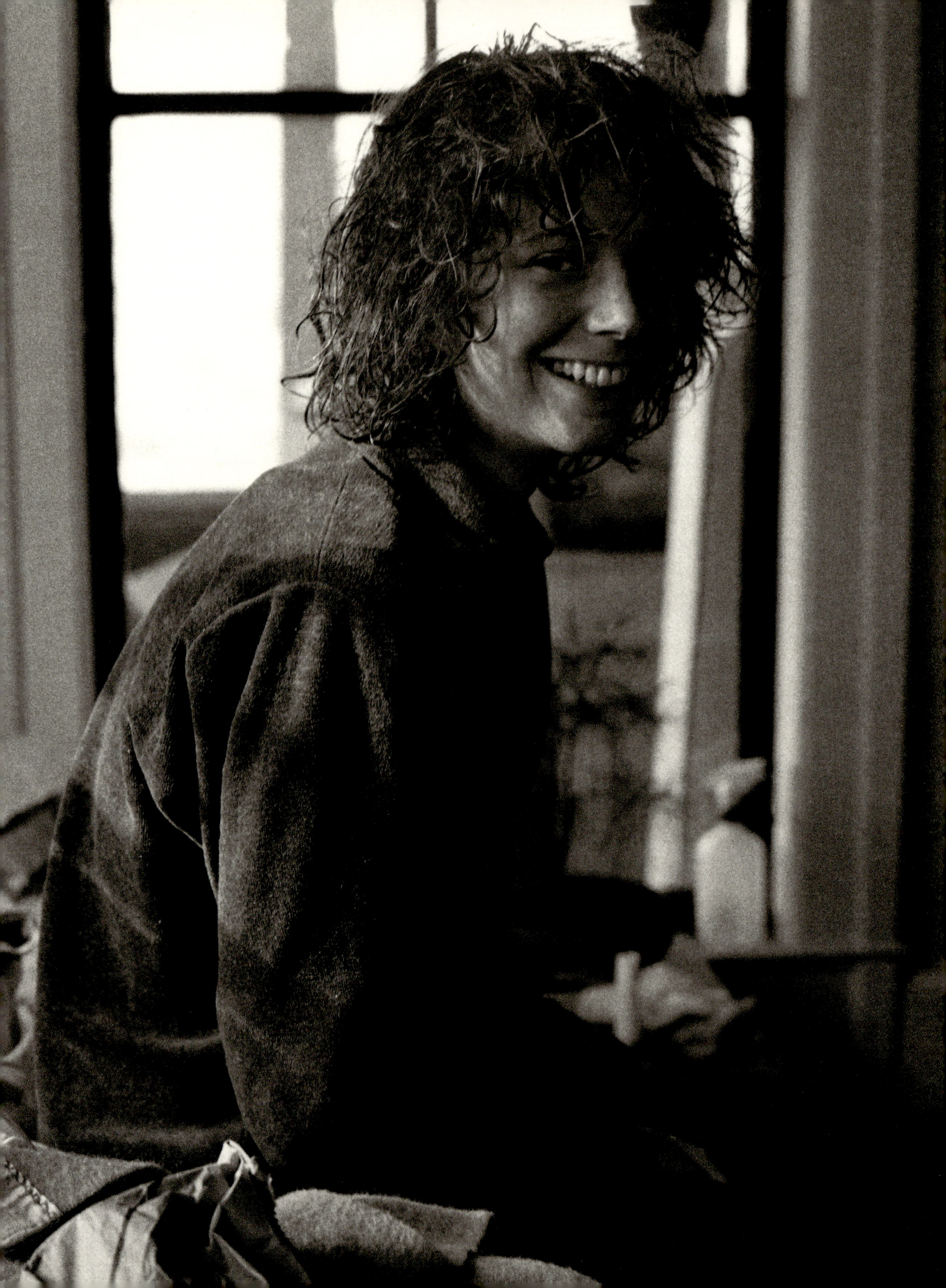

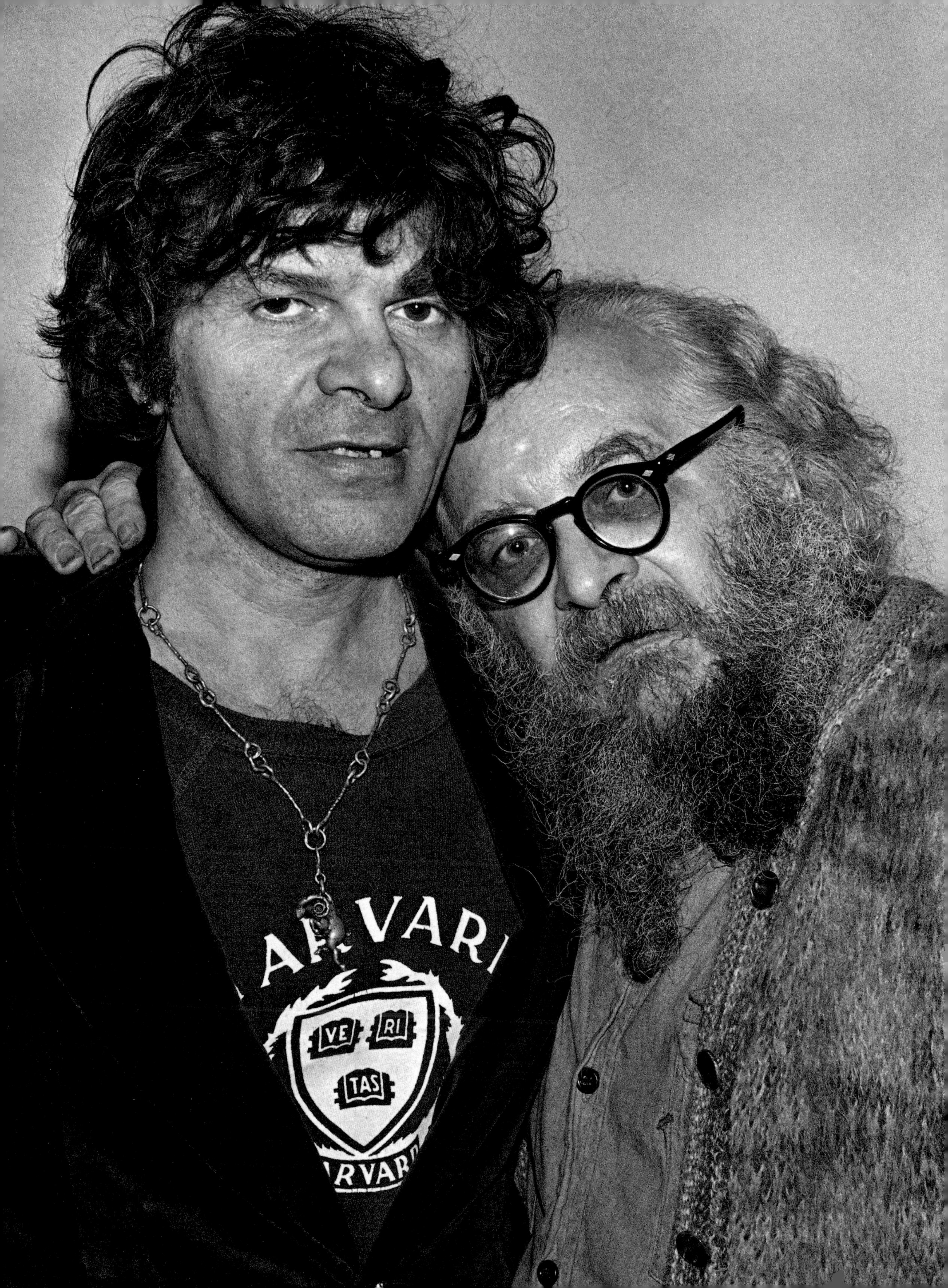
VE
RI
TAS

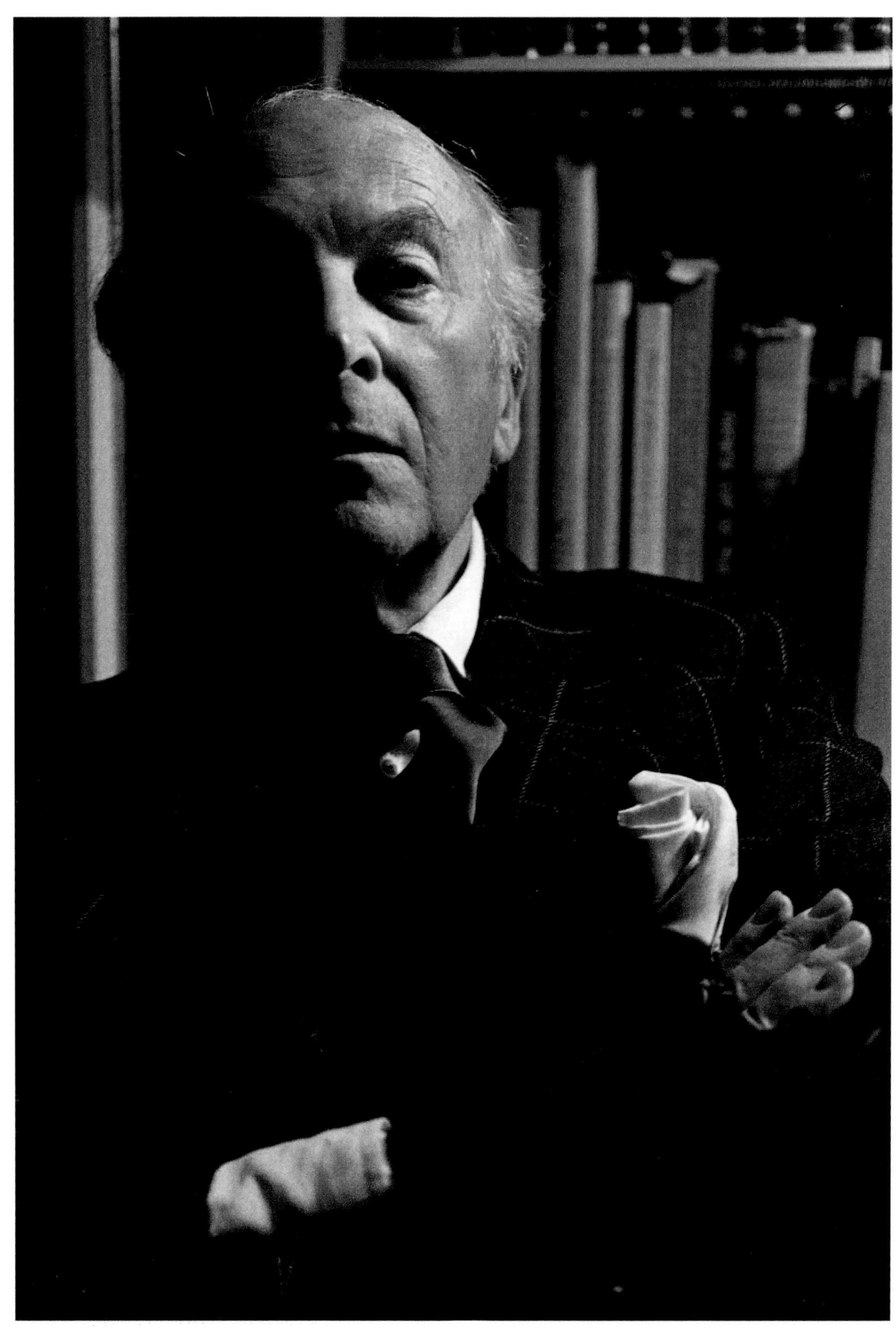

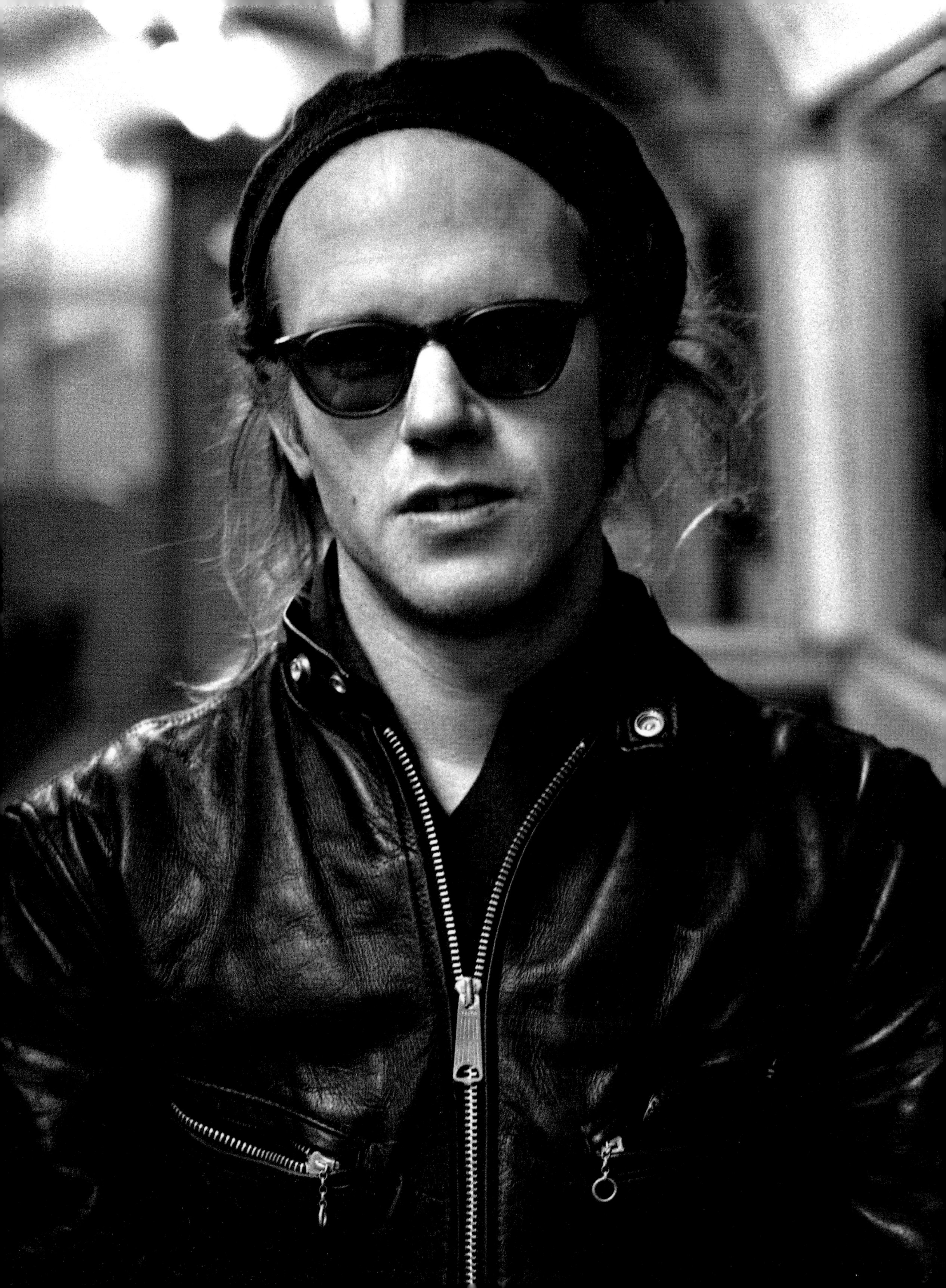

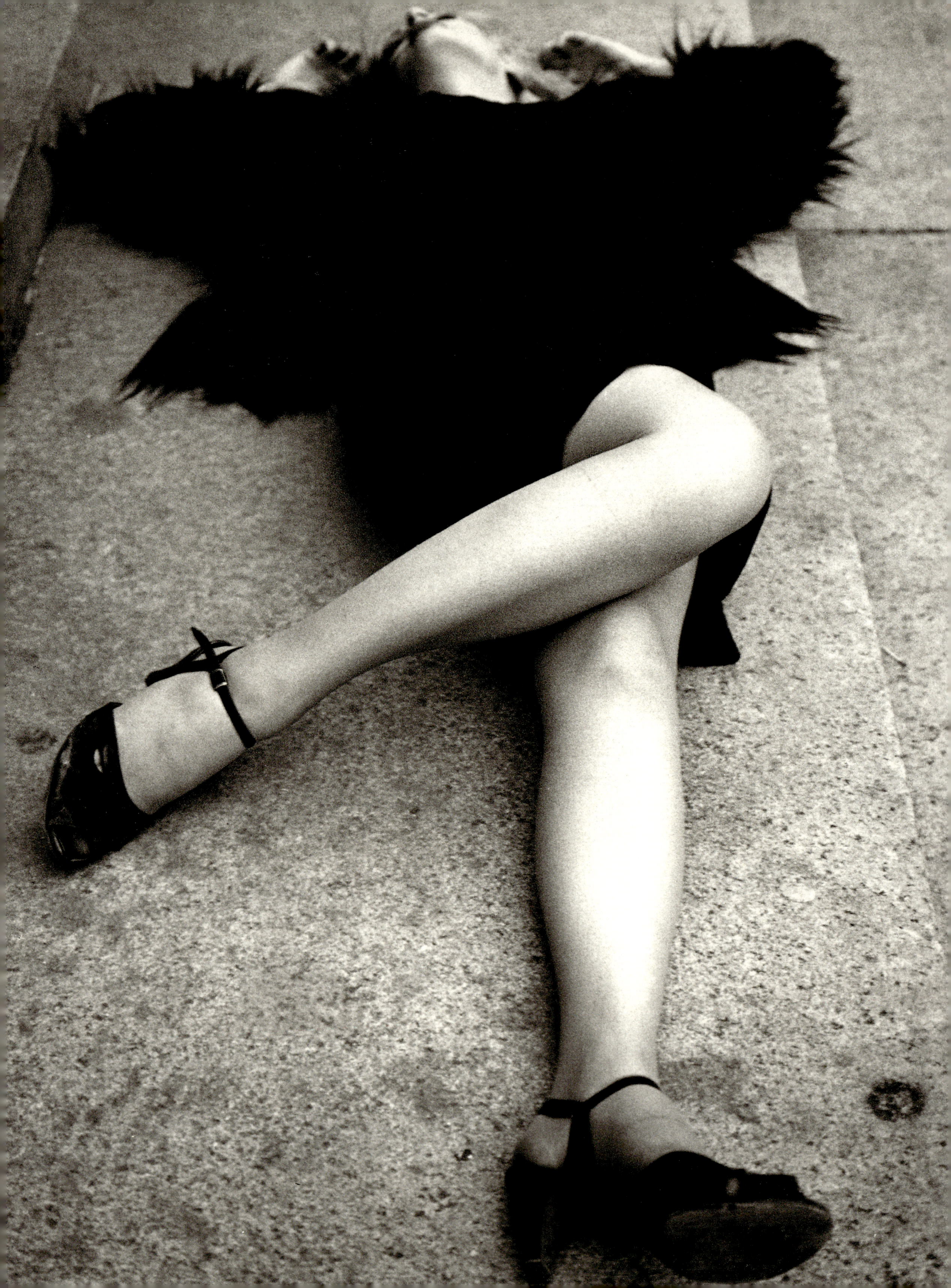

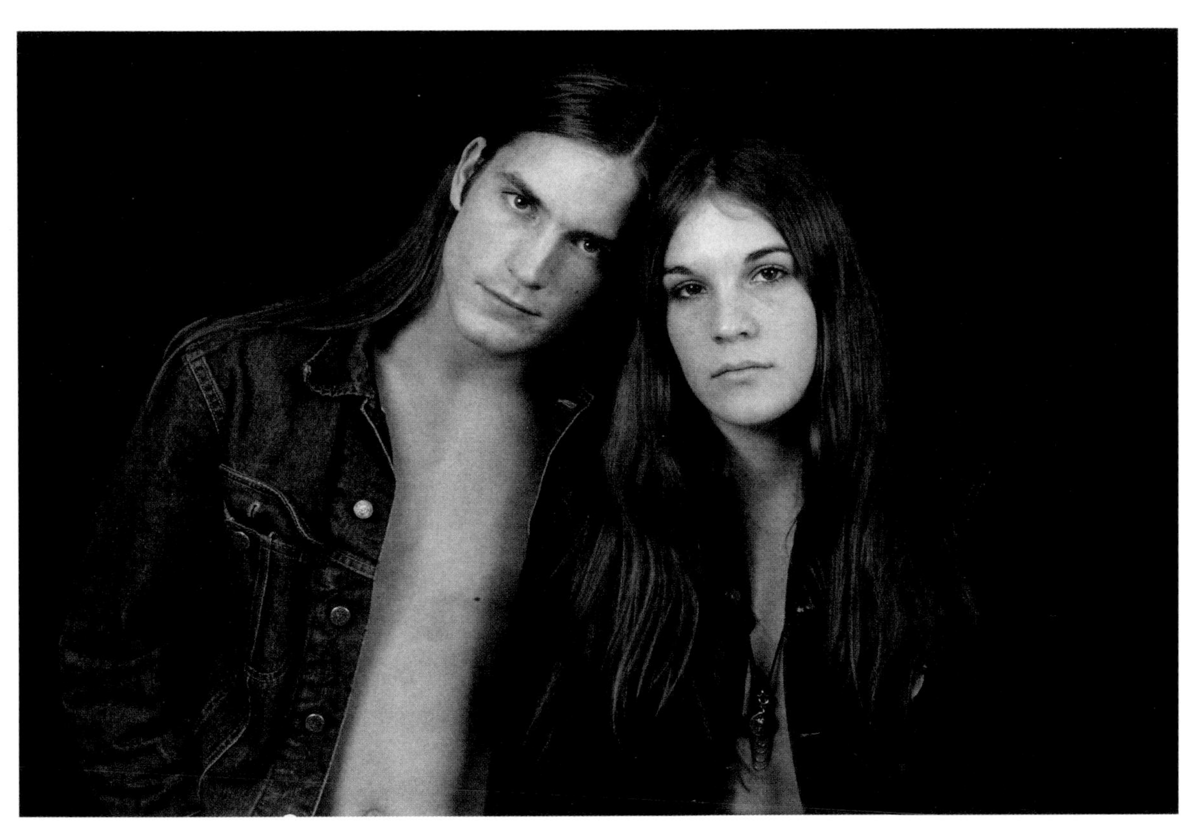

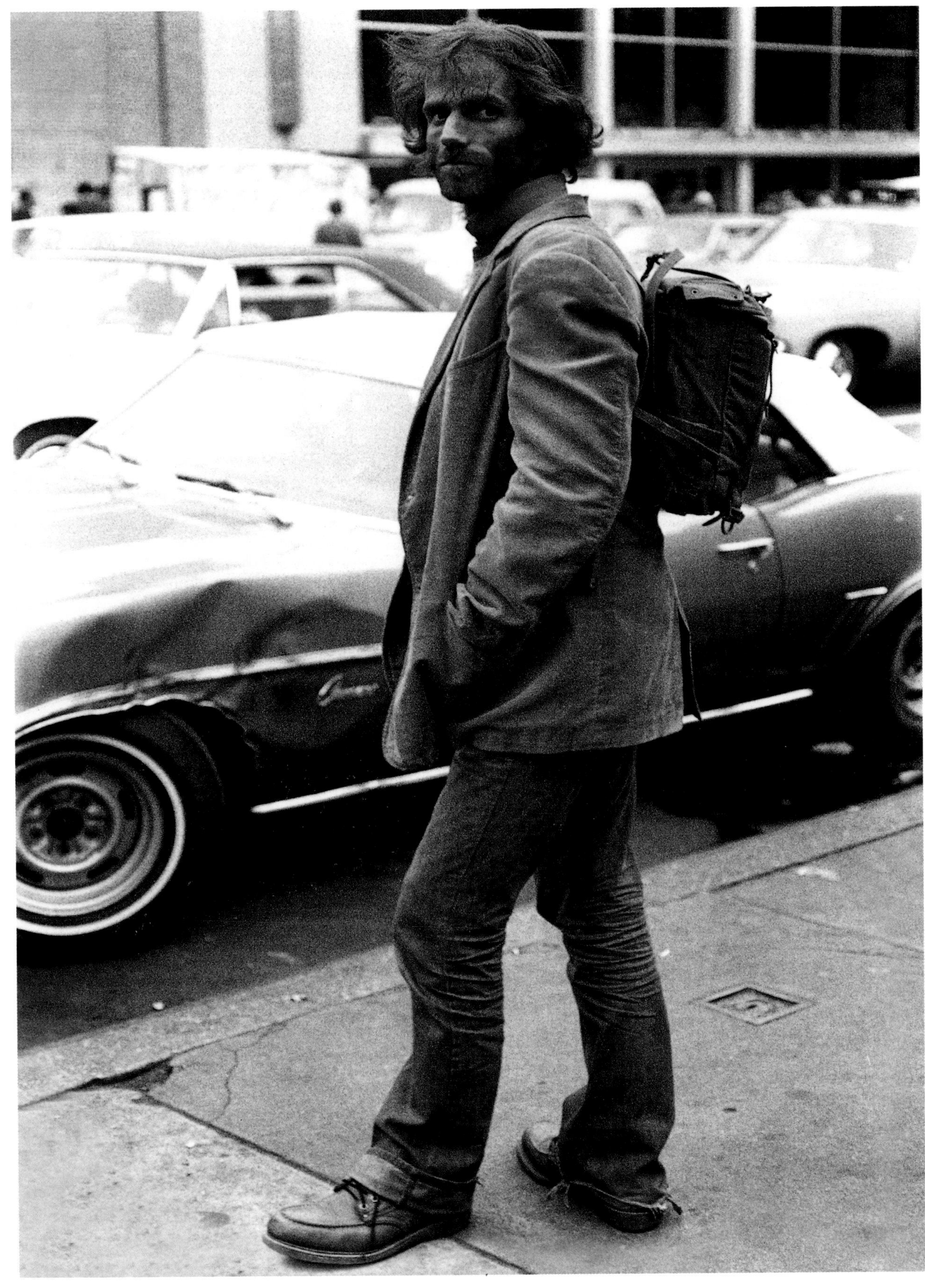

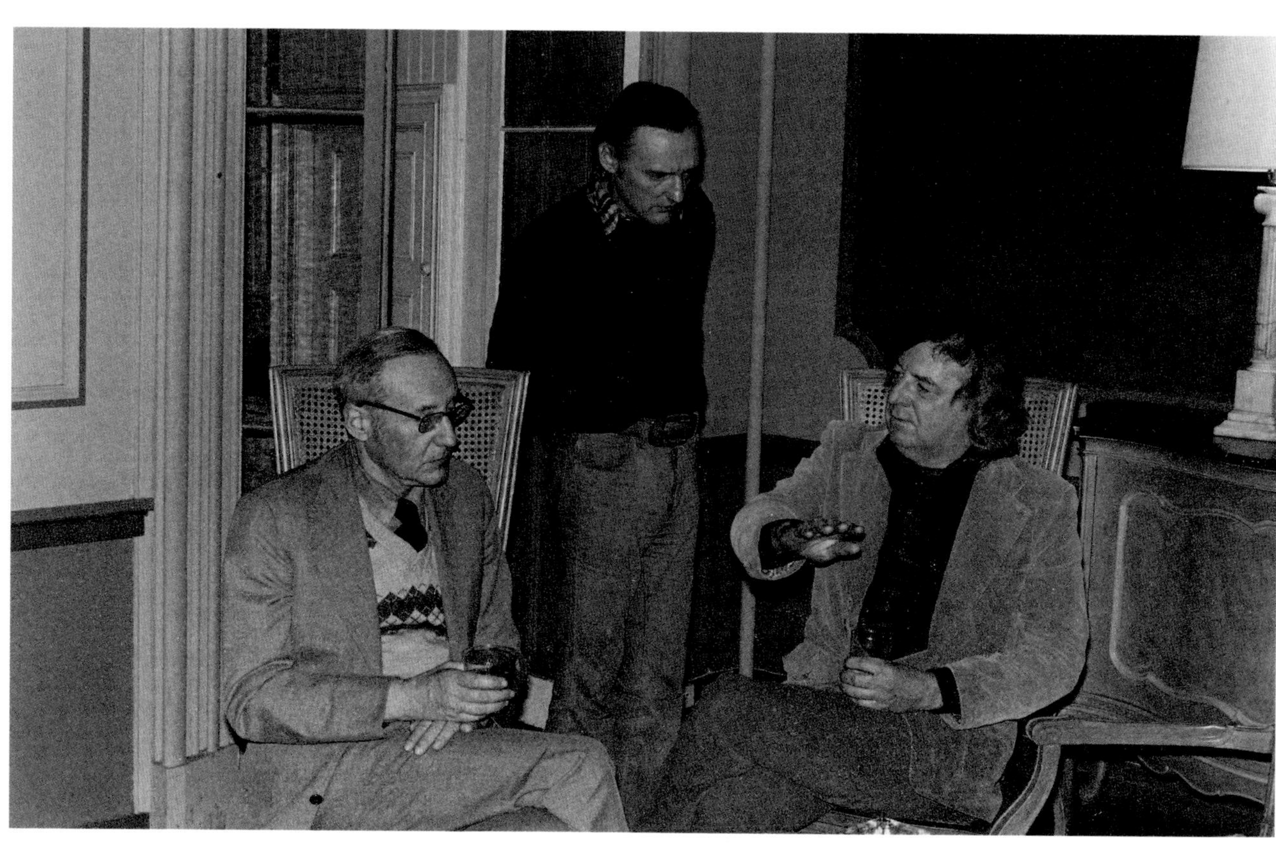

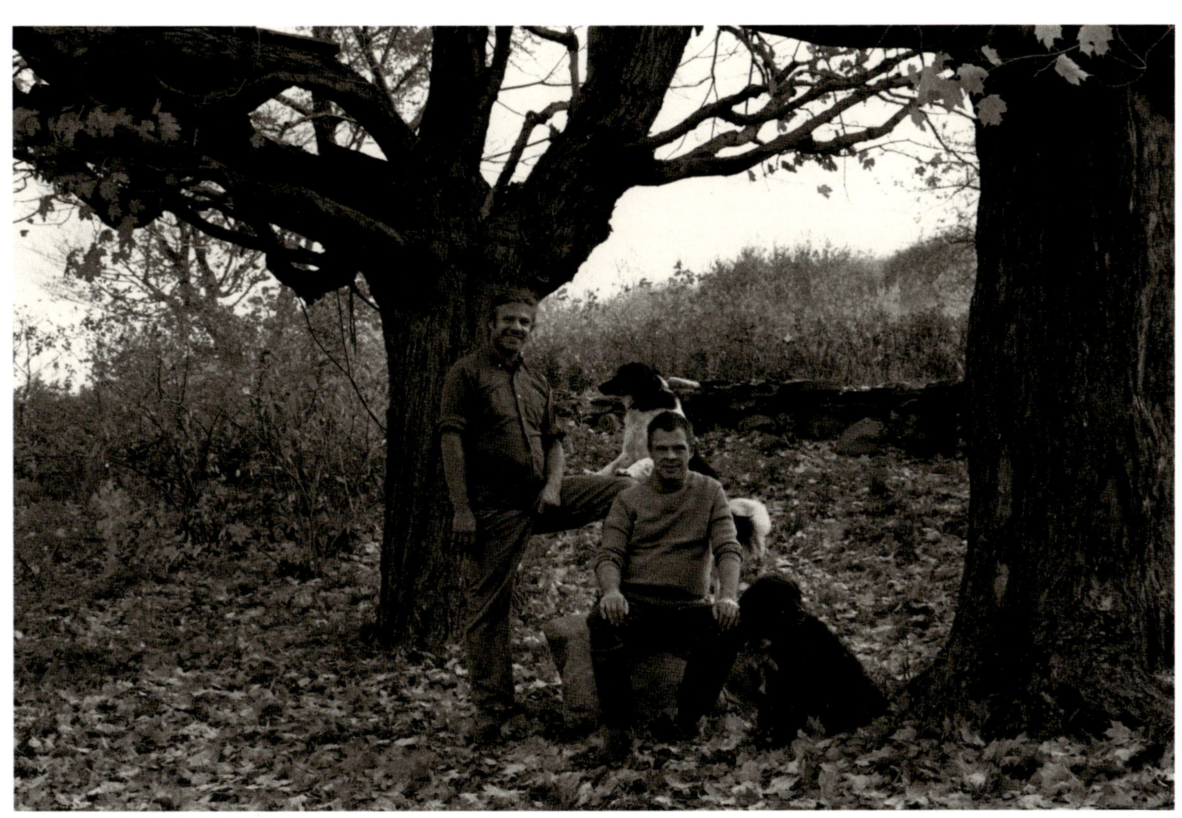

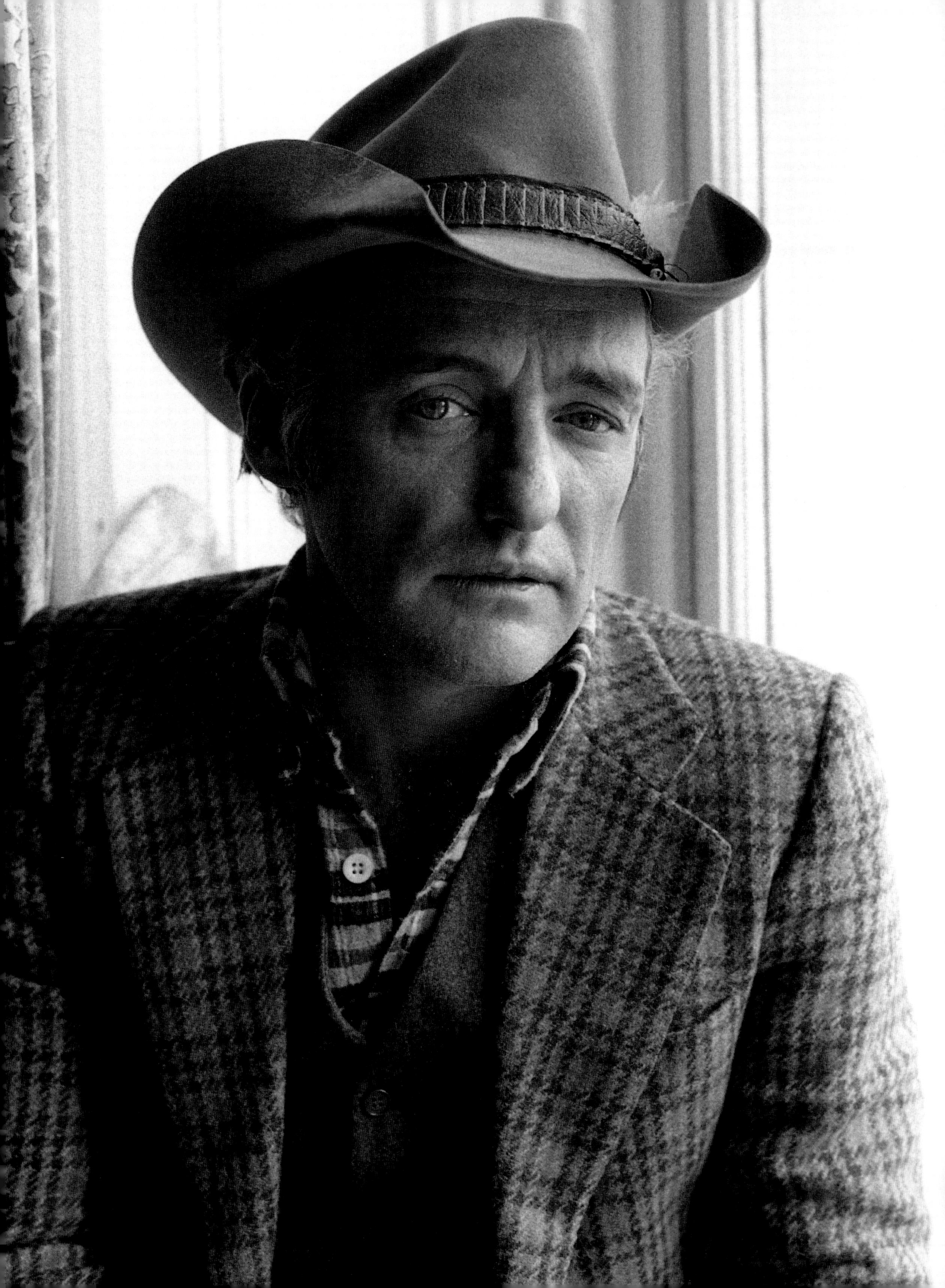

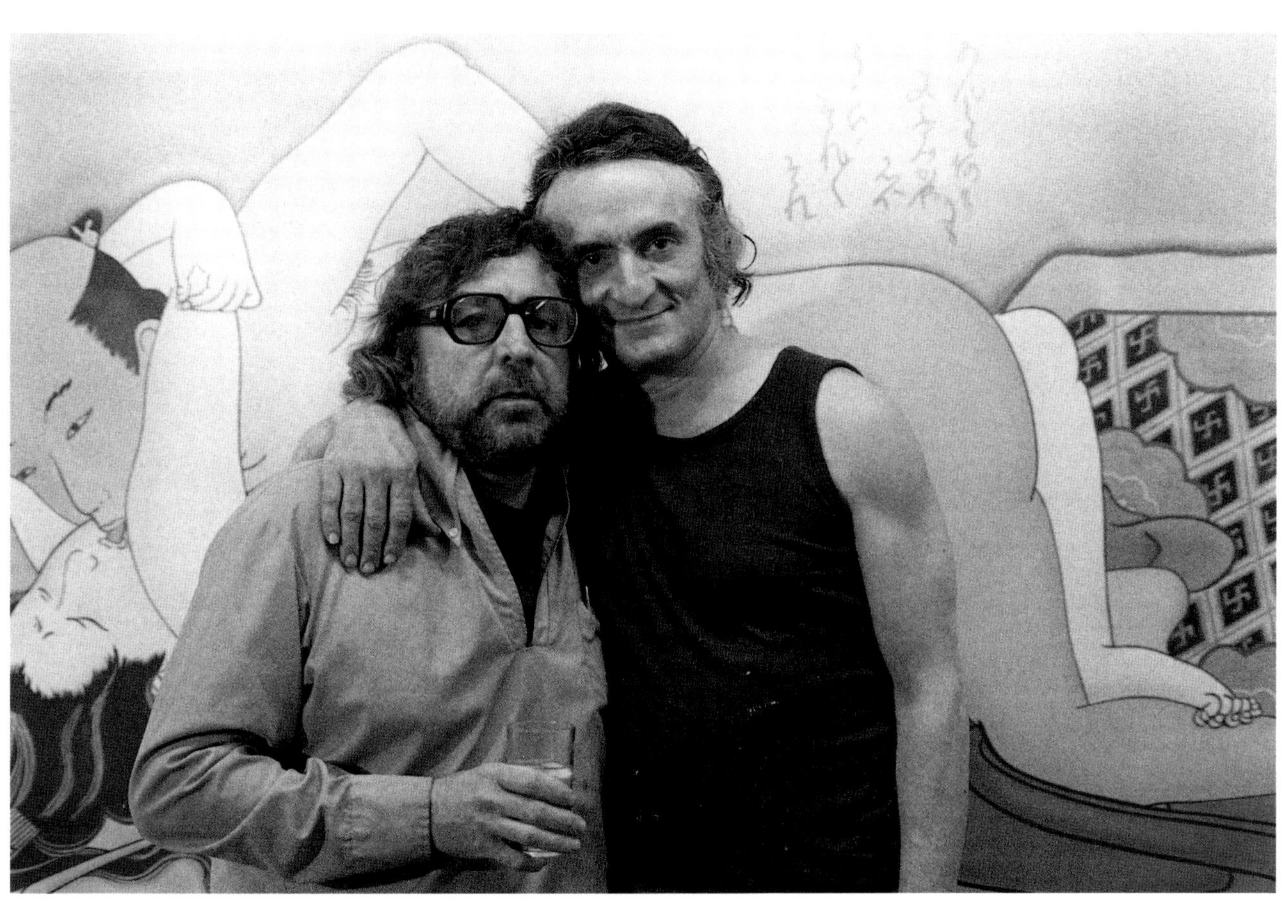

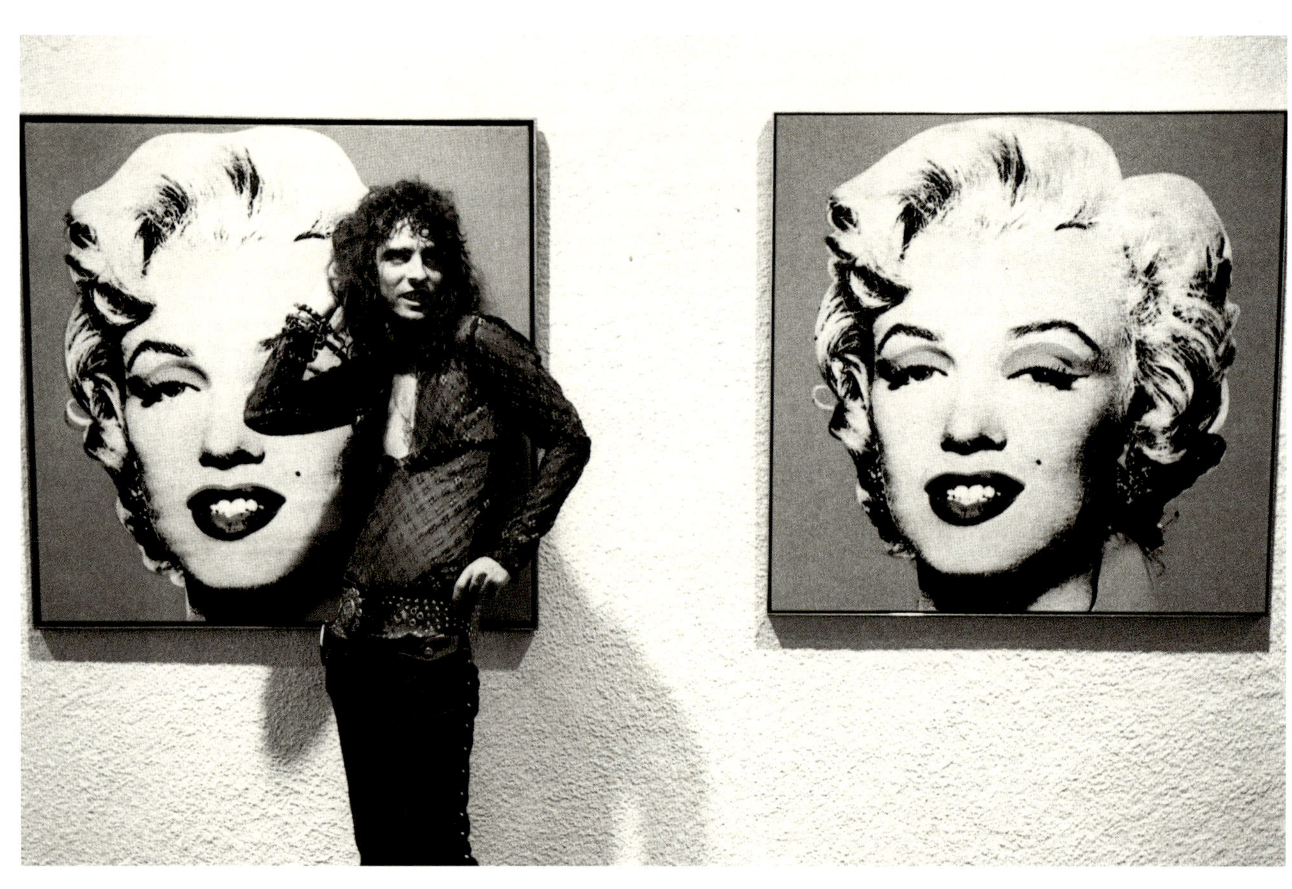

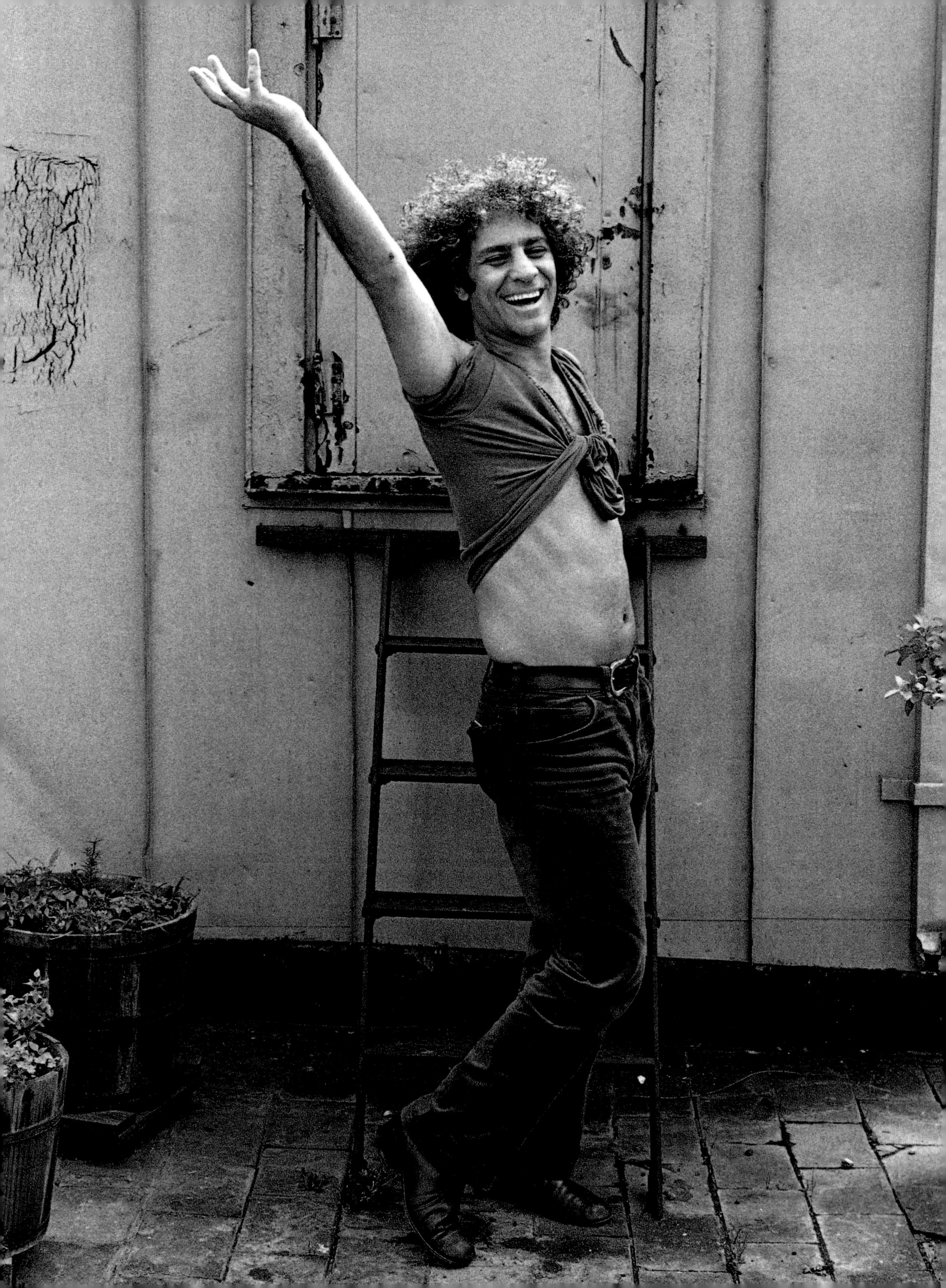

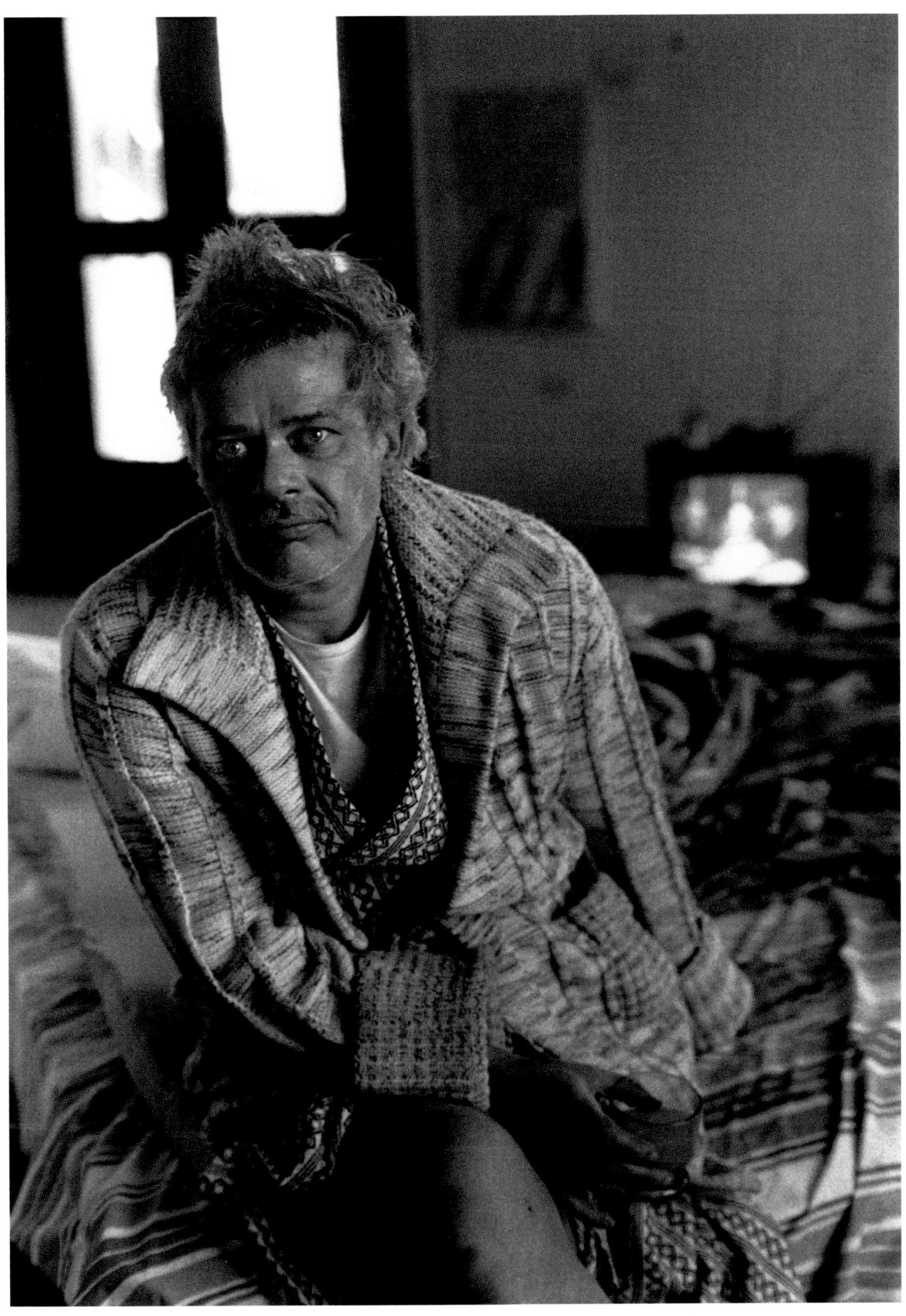

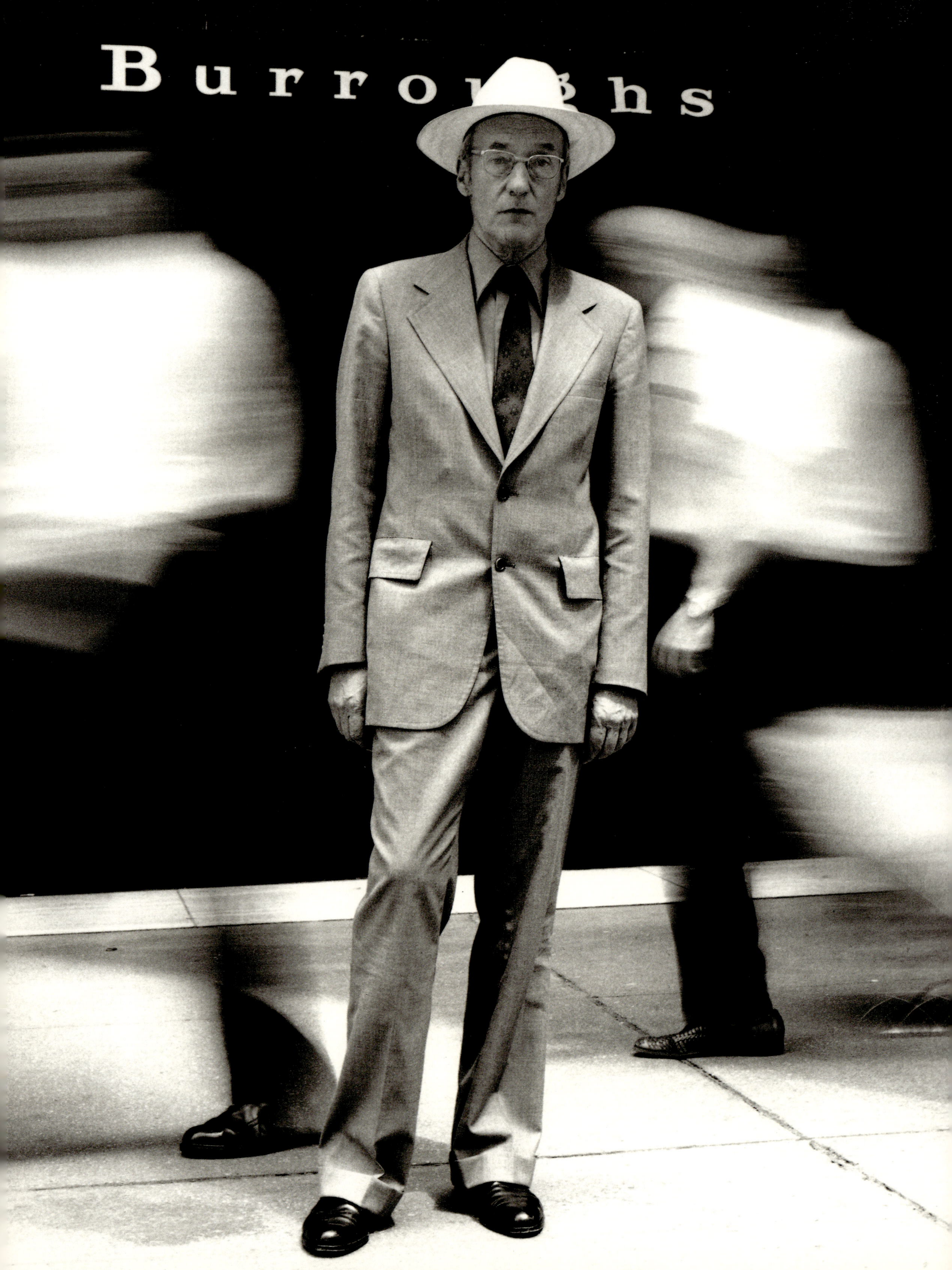
Burroughs

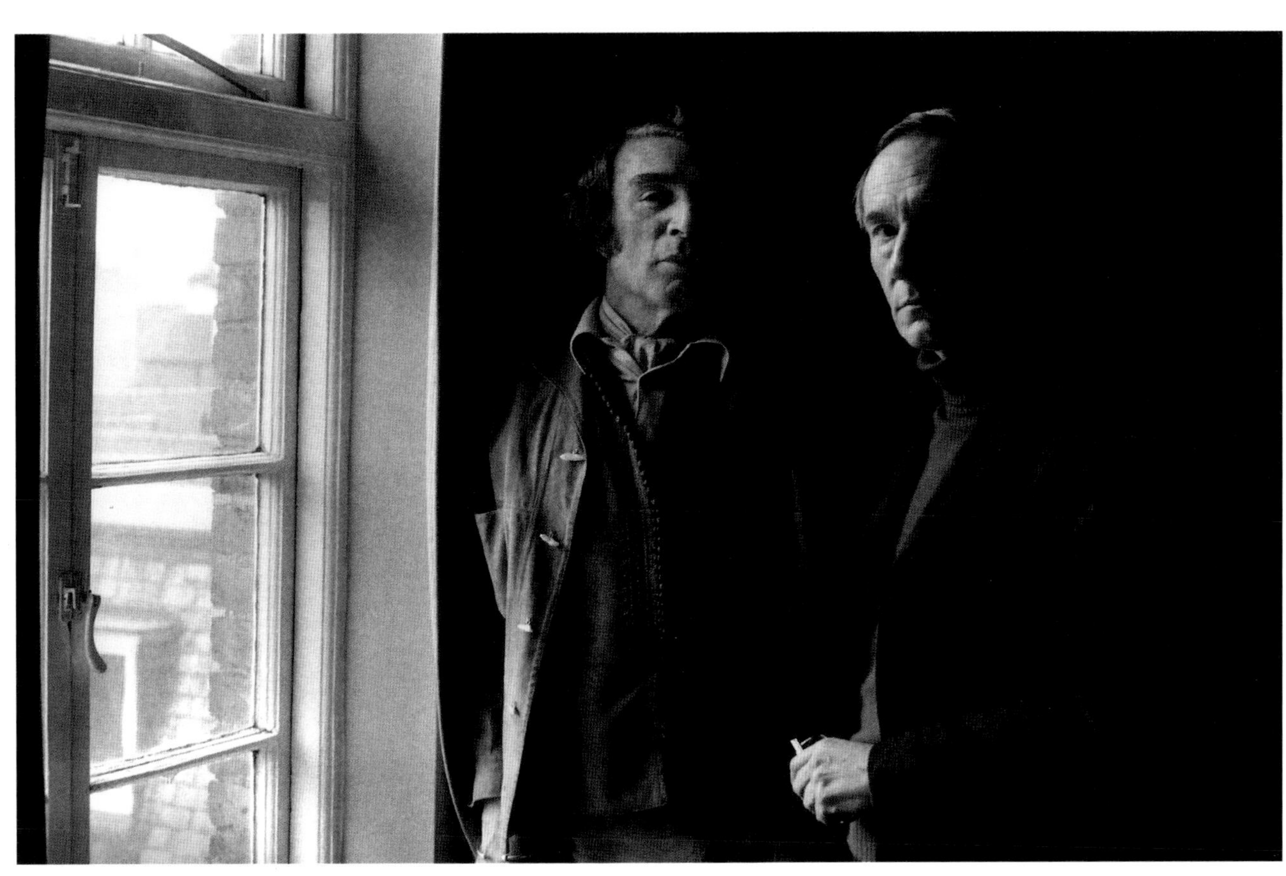

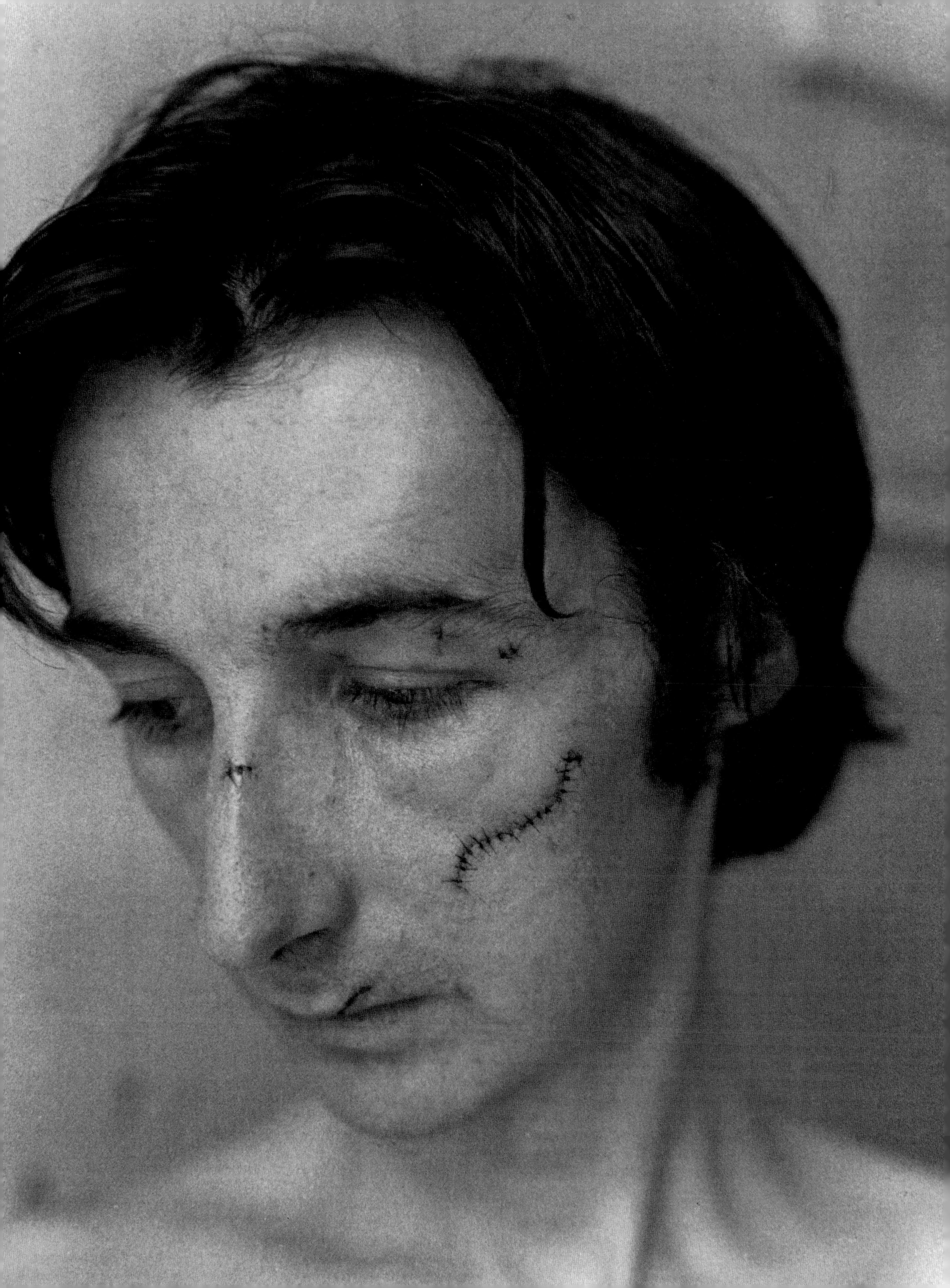

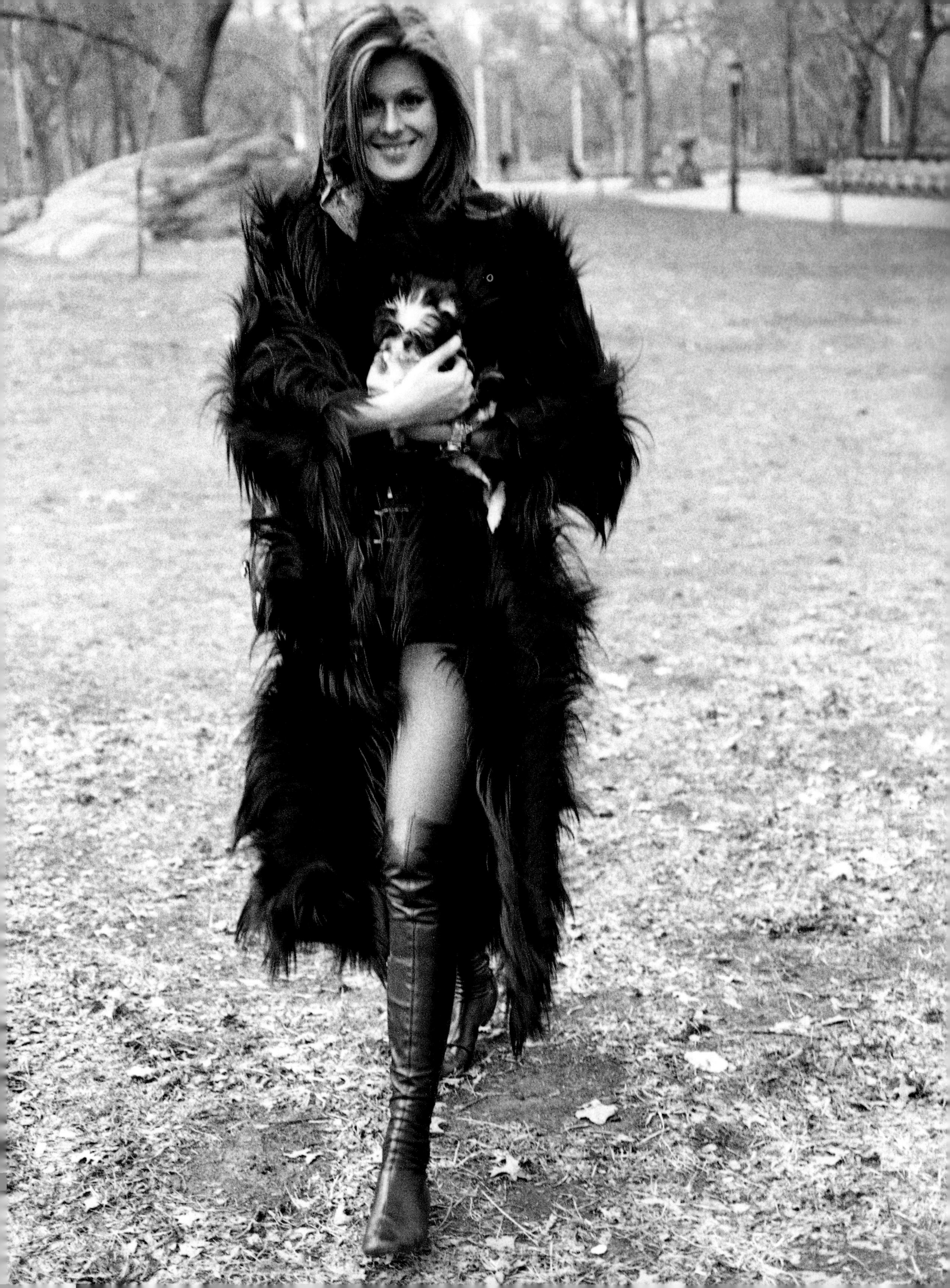

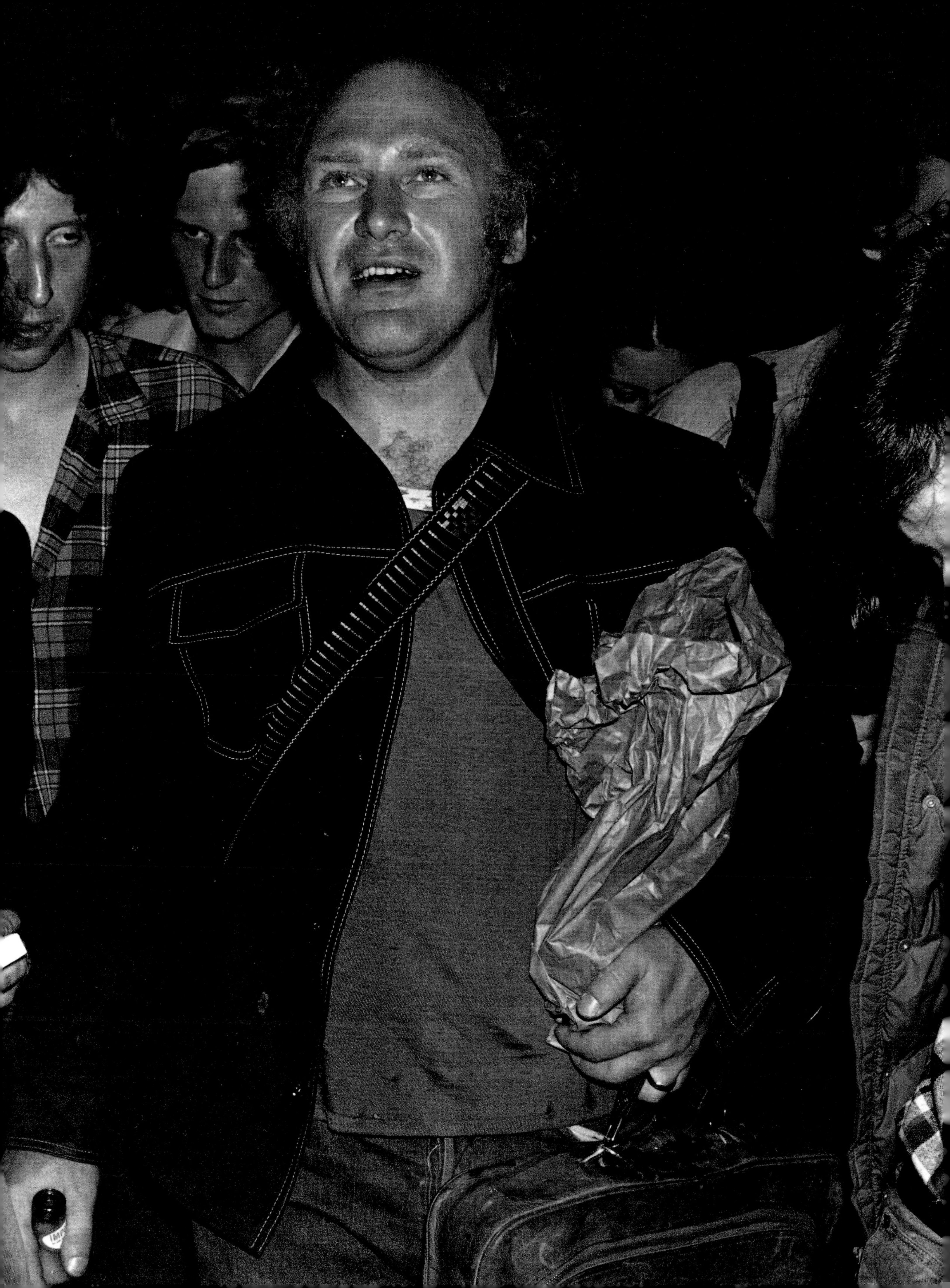

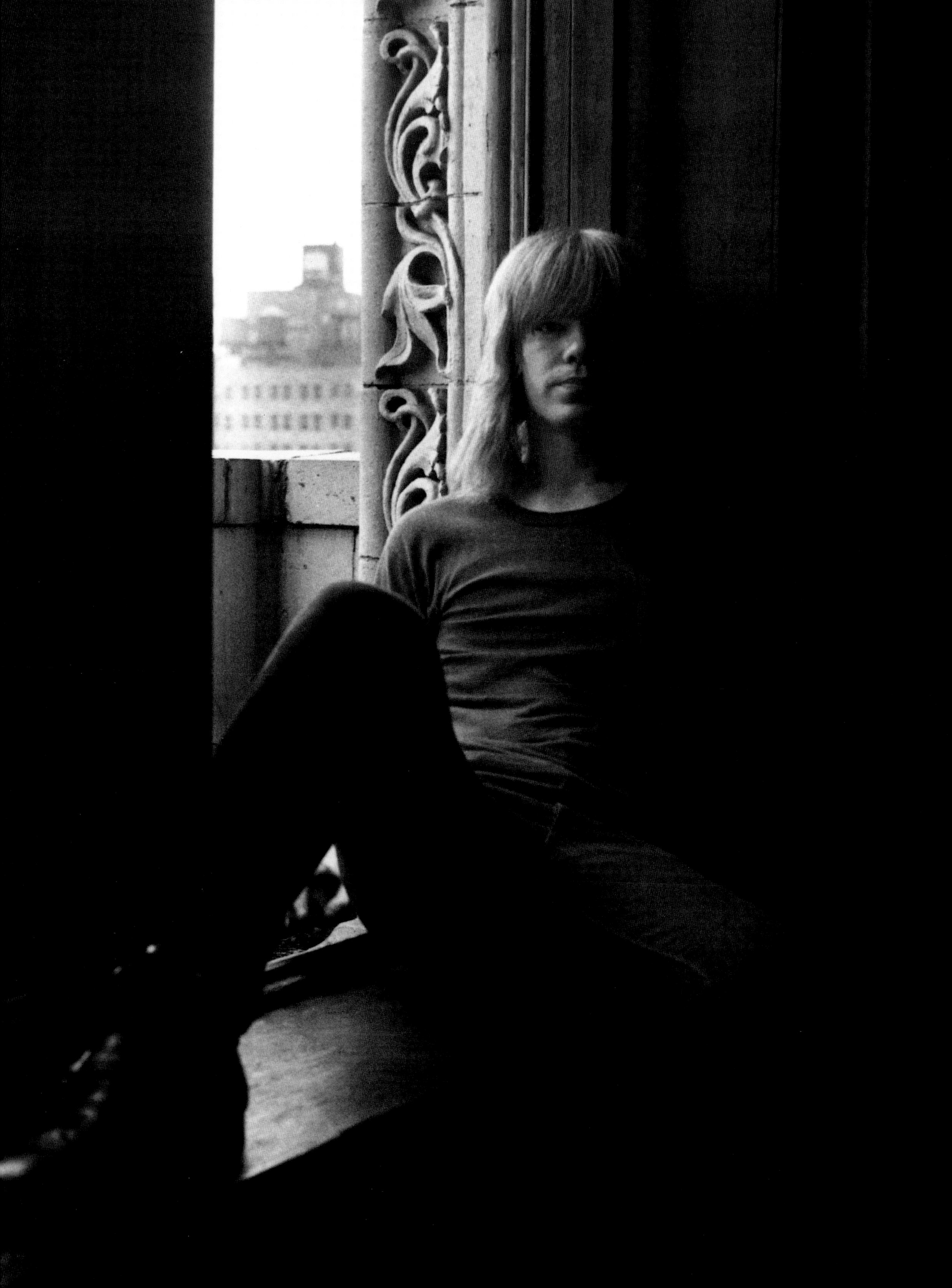

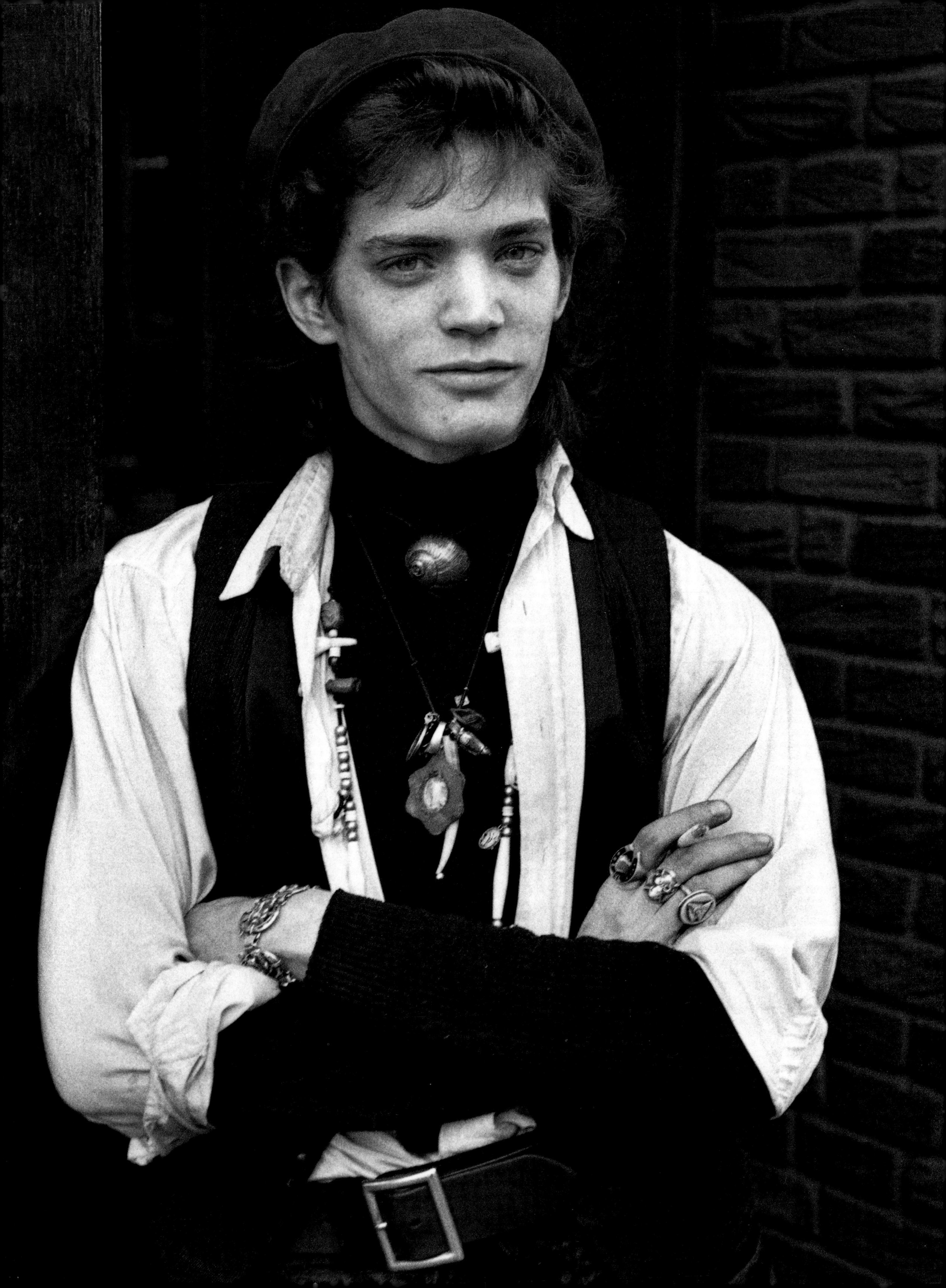

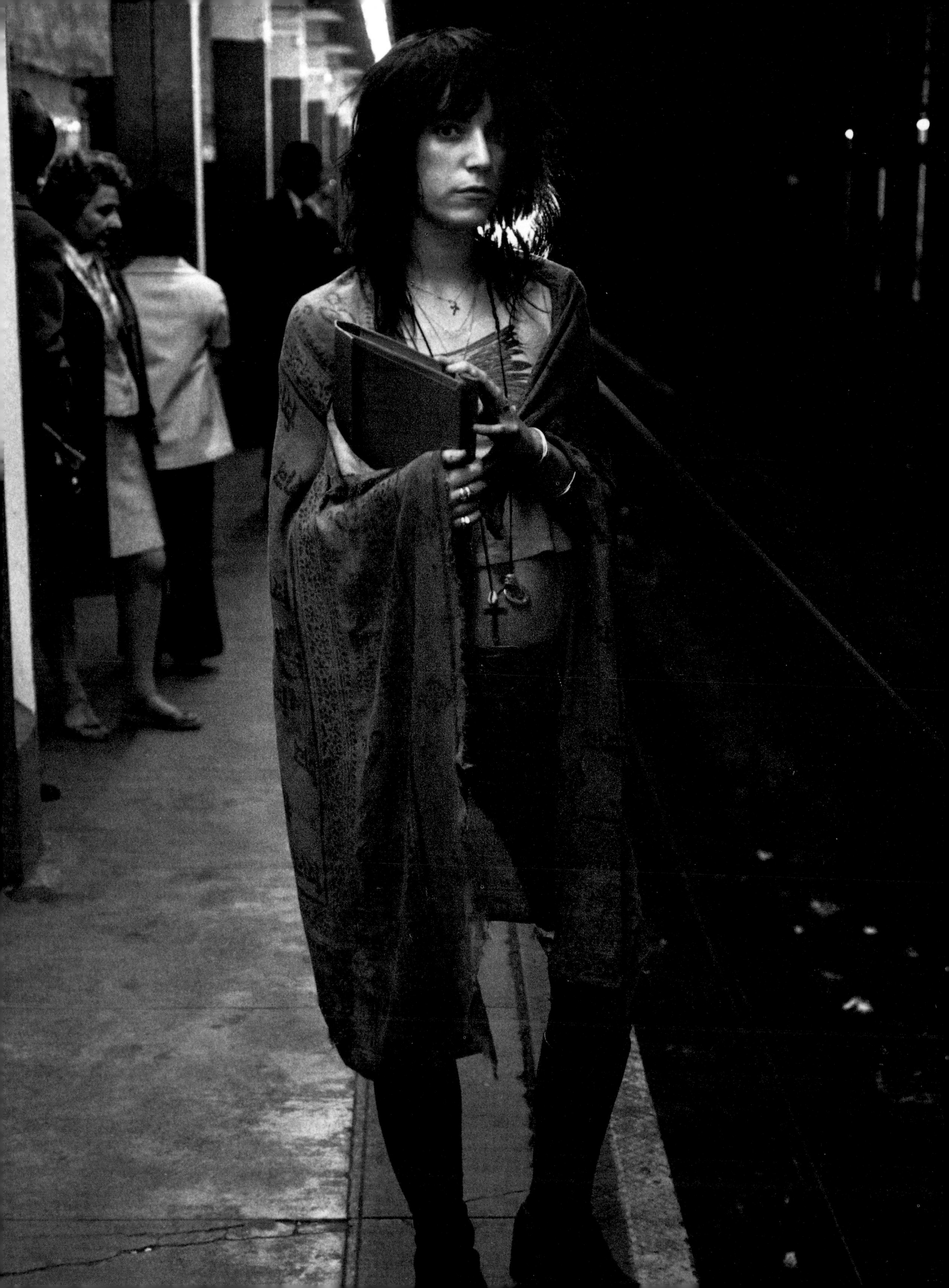

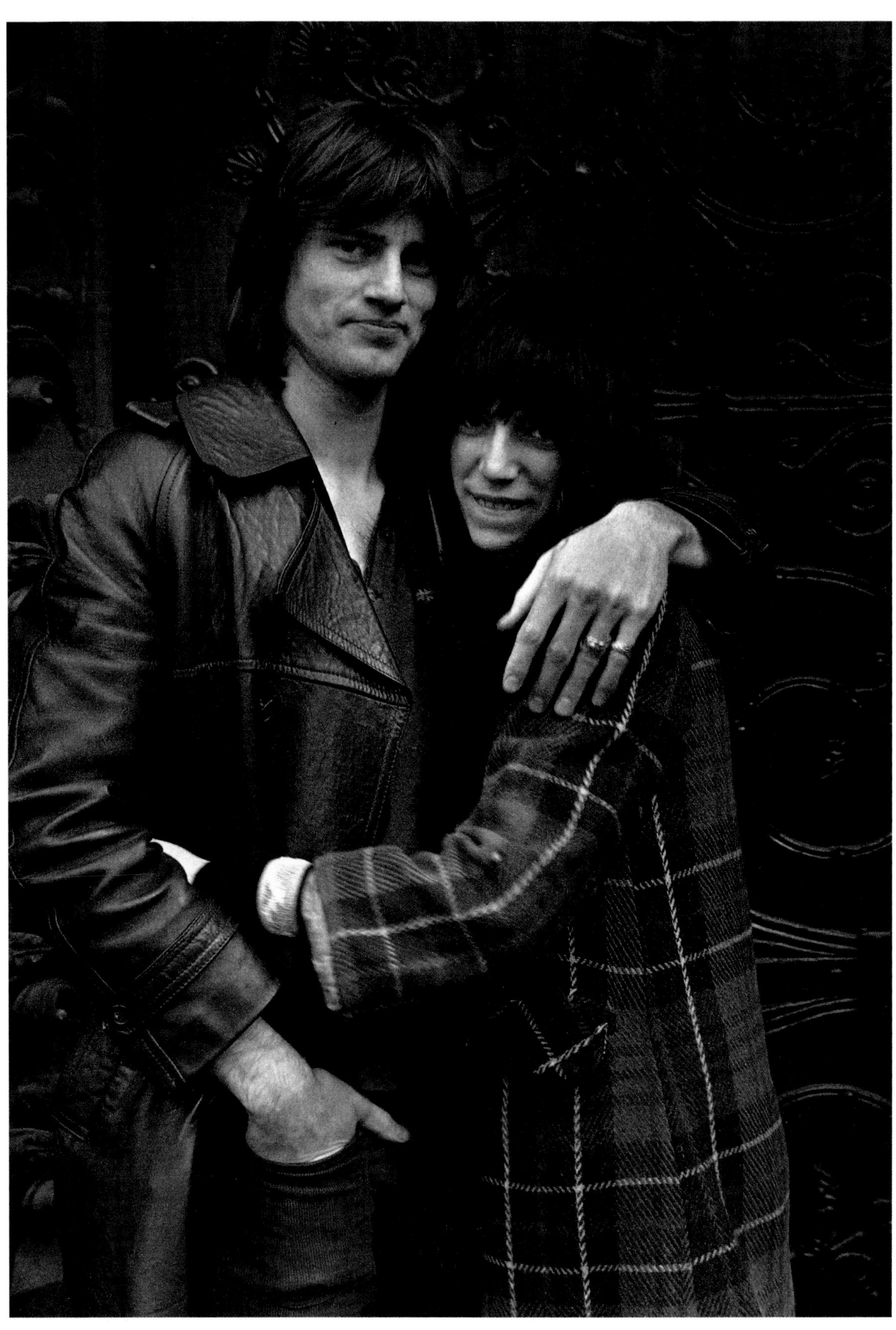

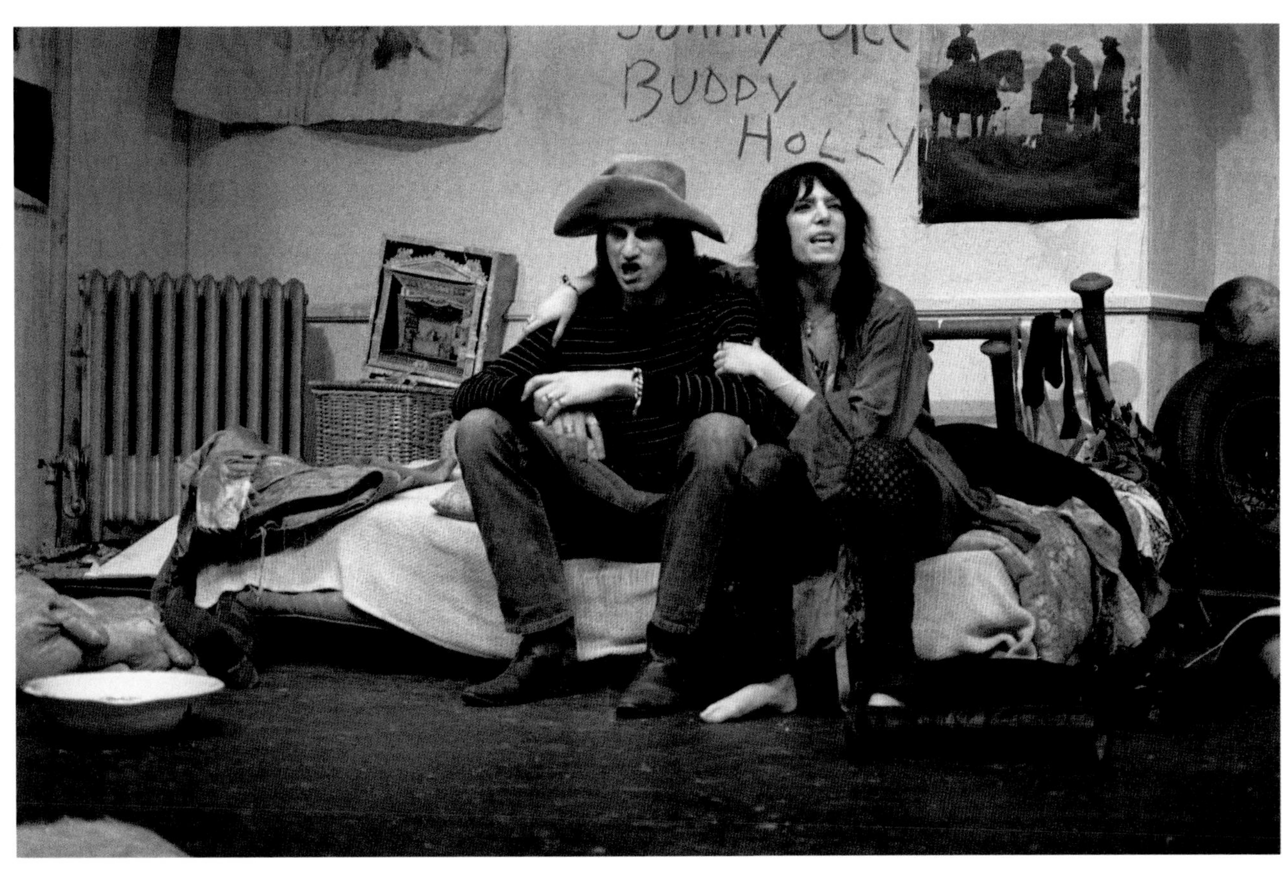
BUDDY
HOLLY

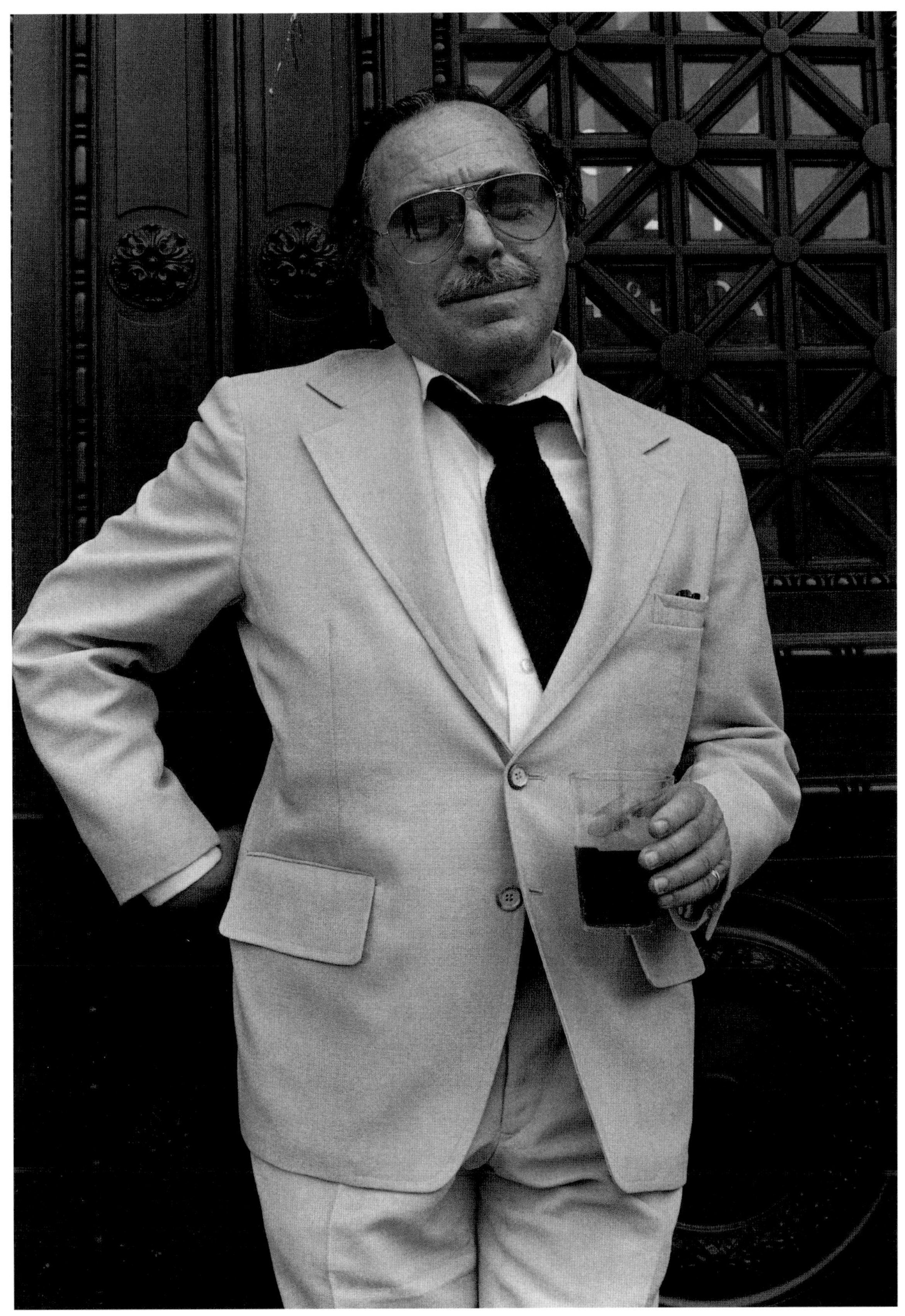

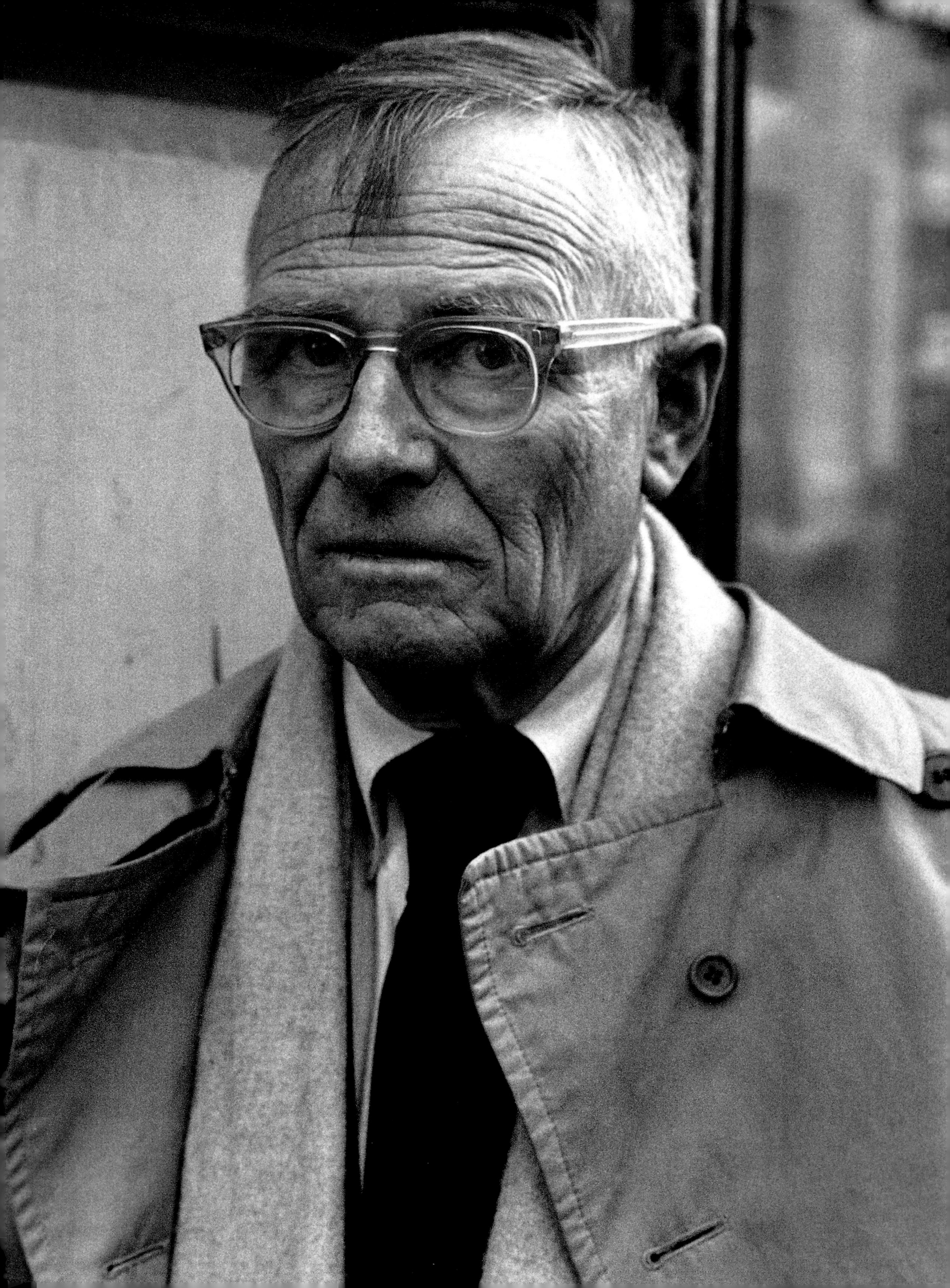

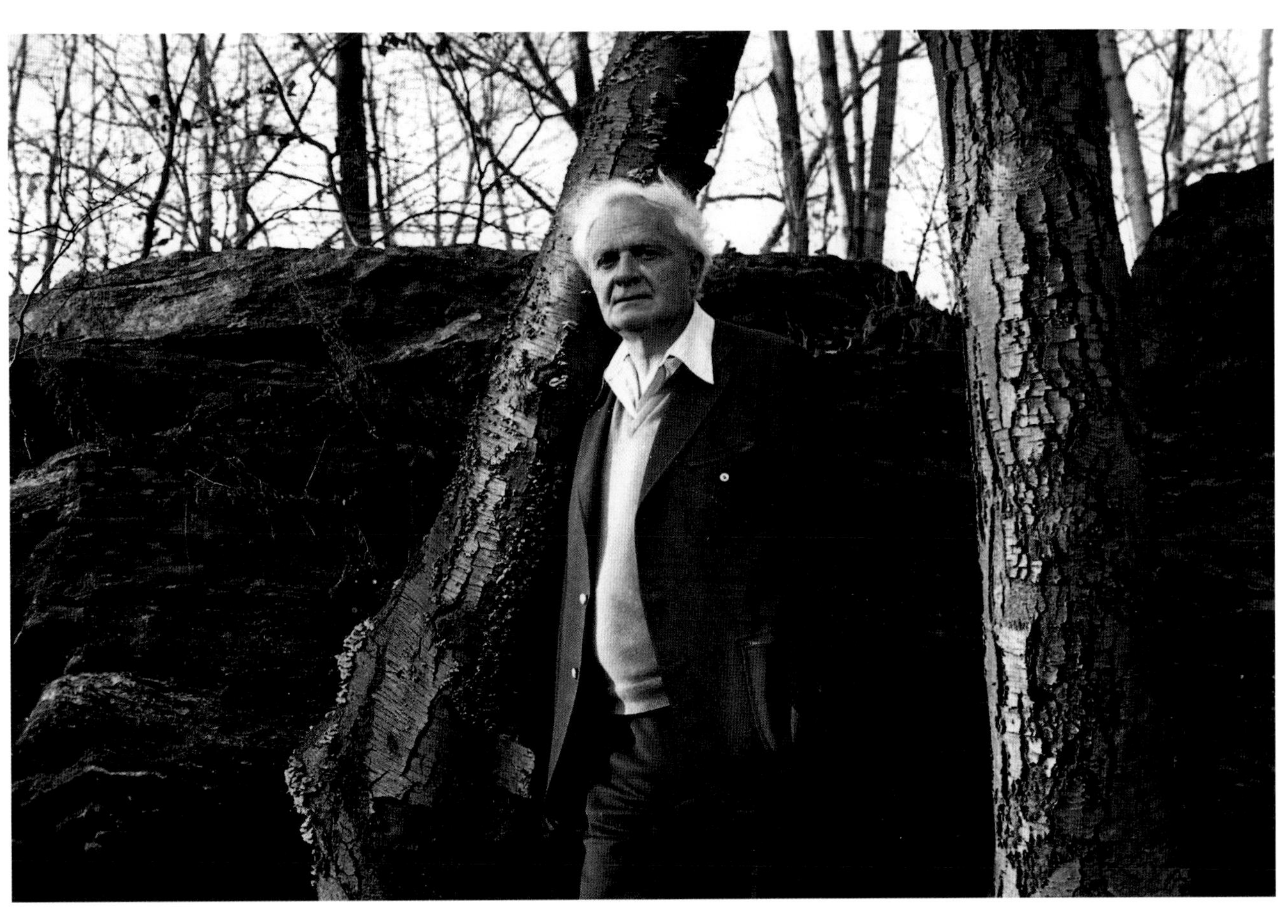

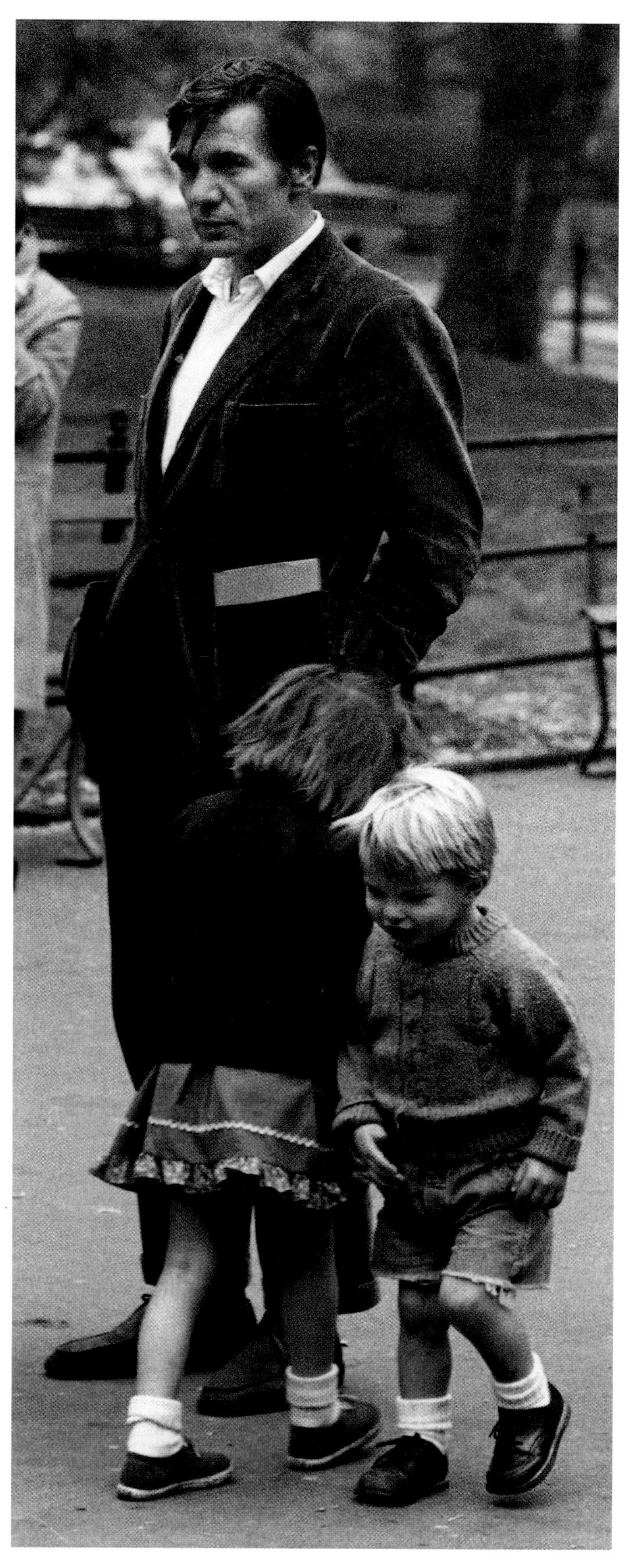

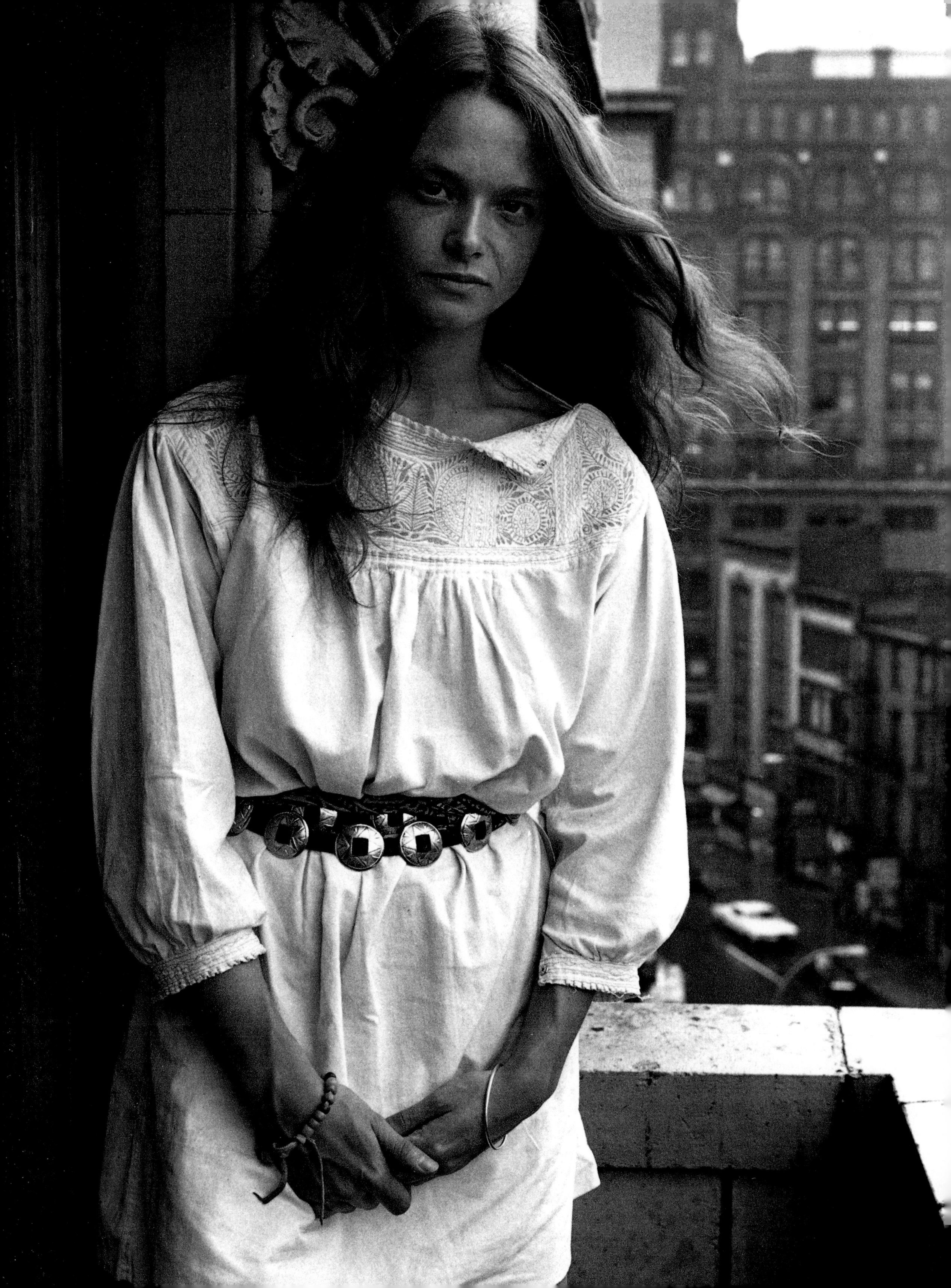

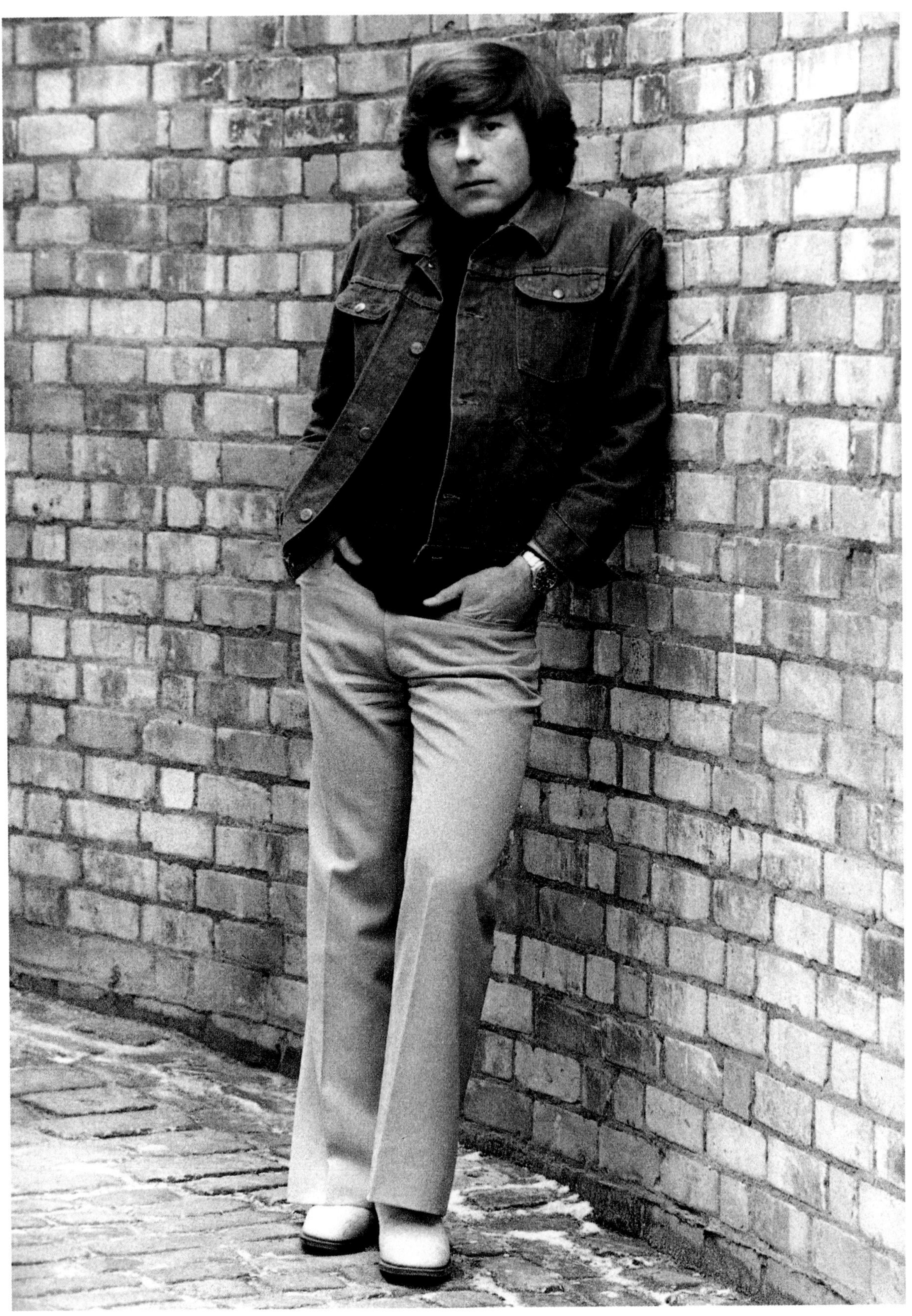

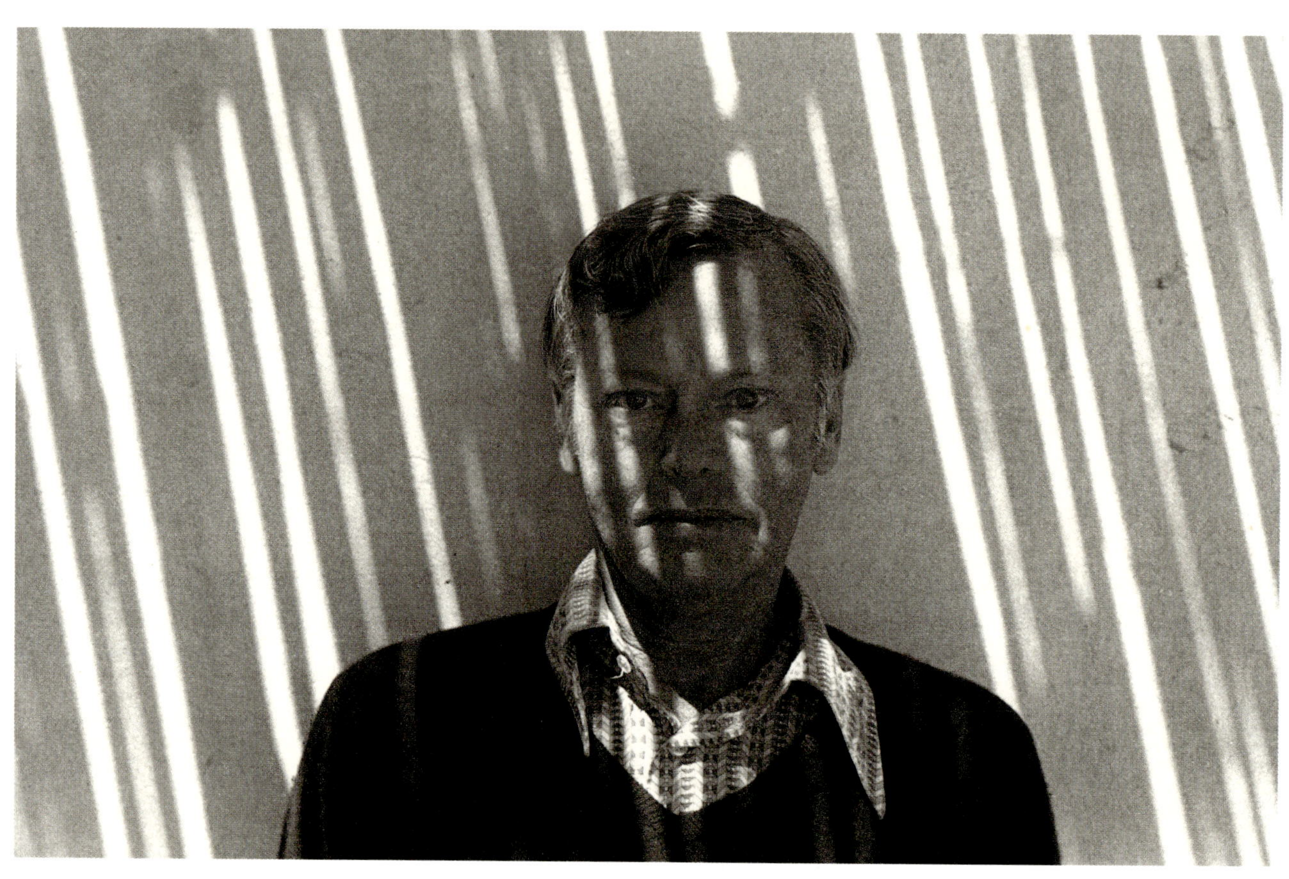

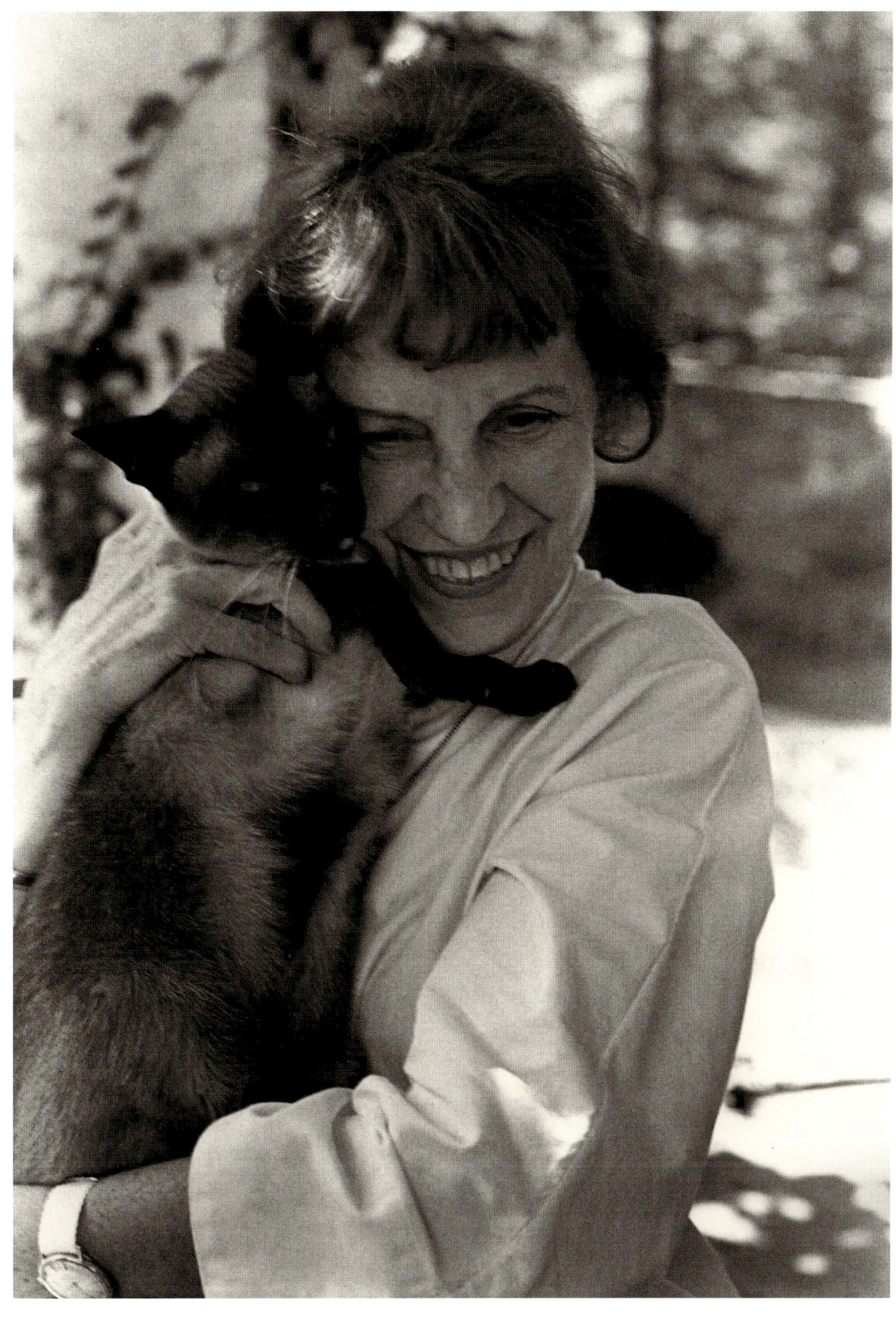

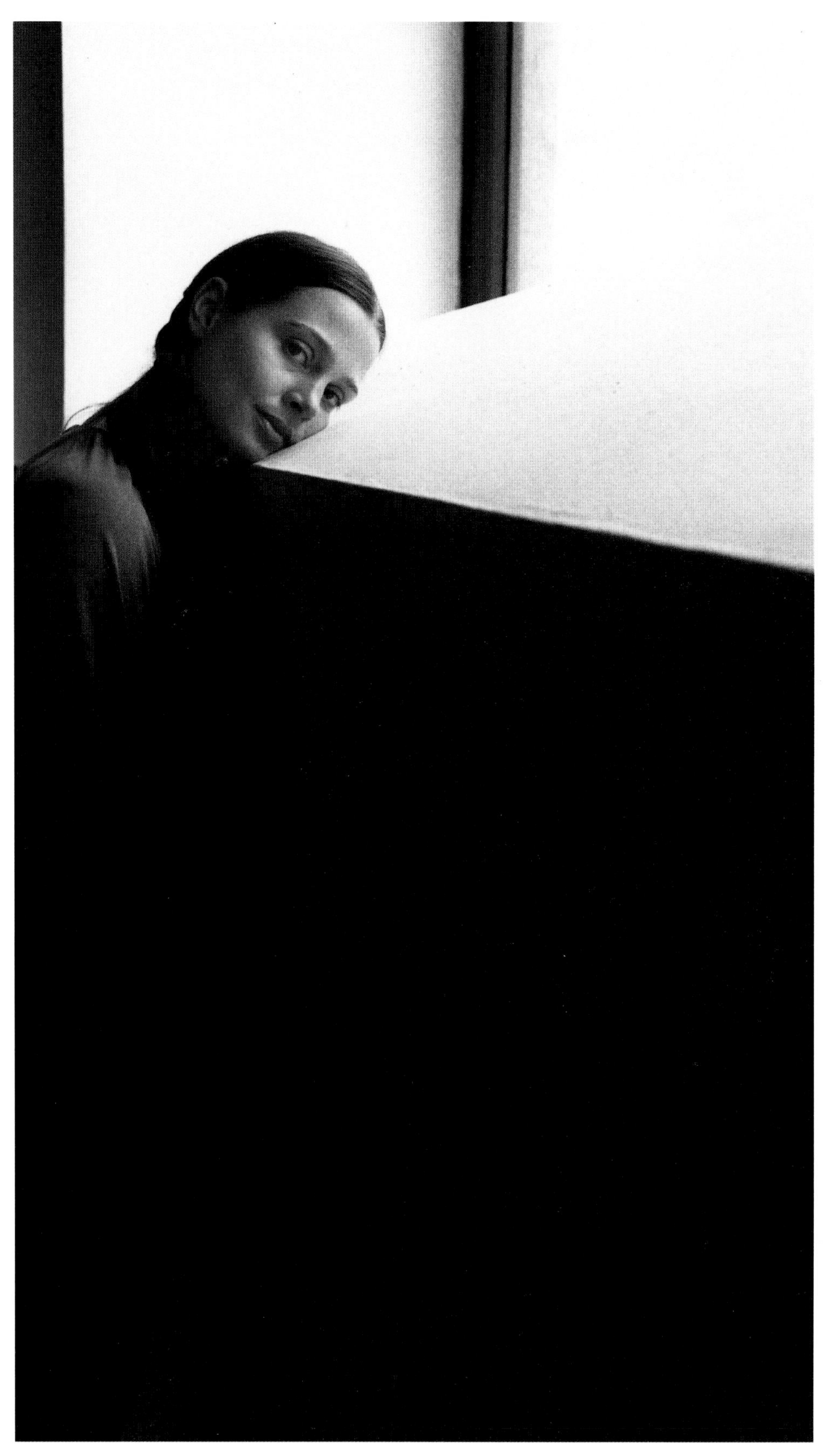

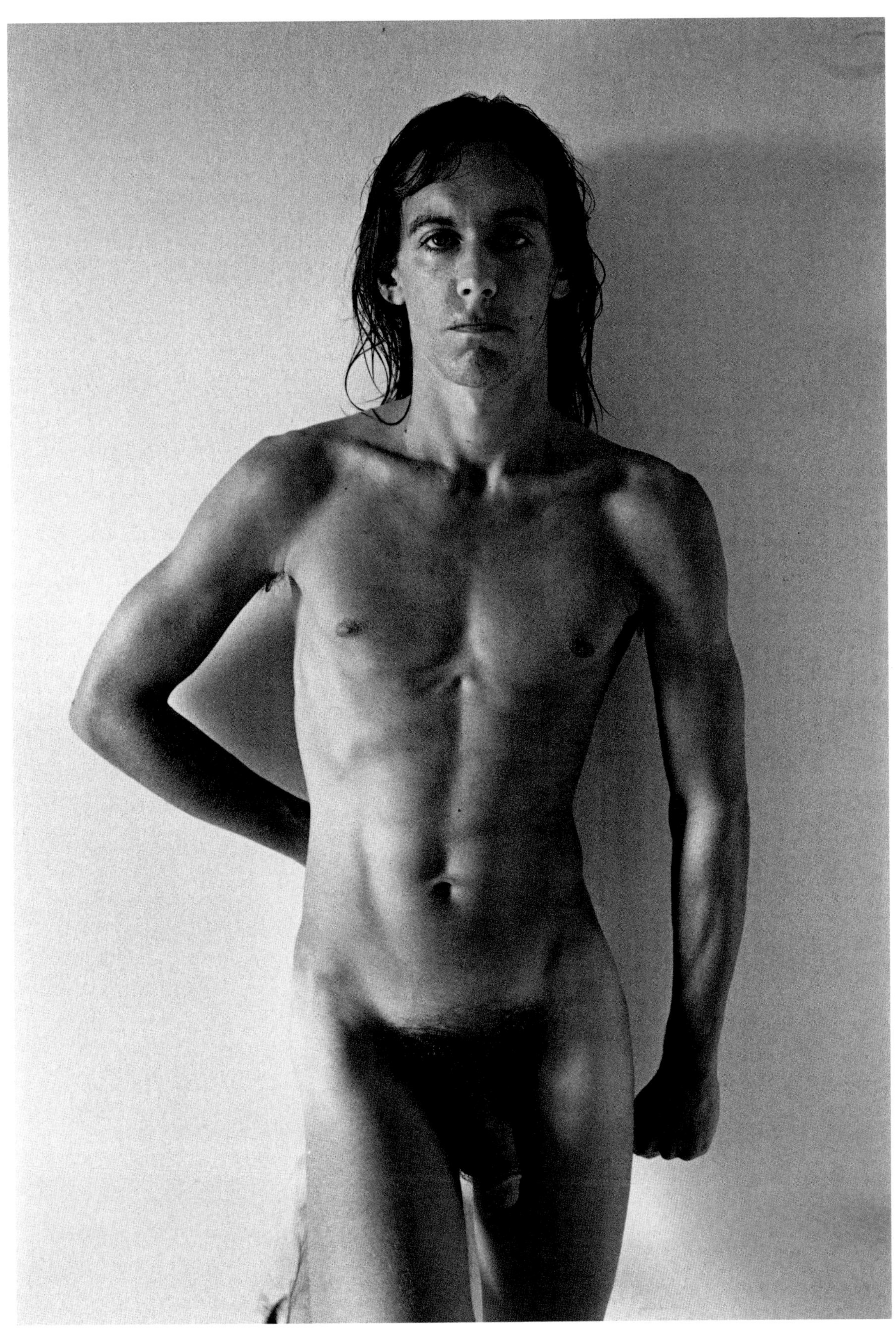

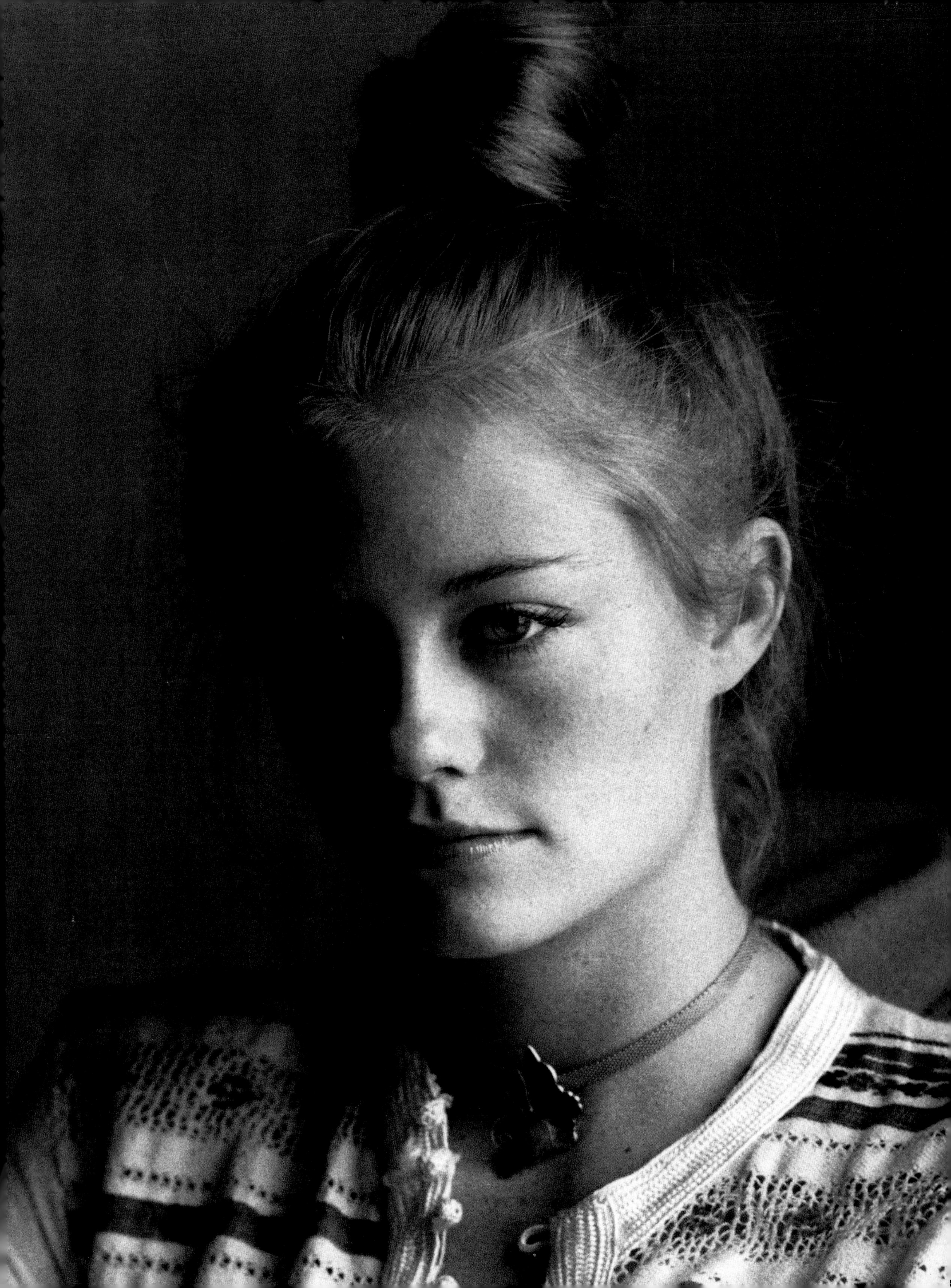

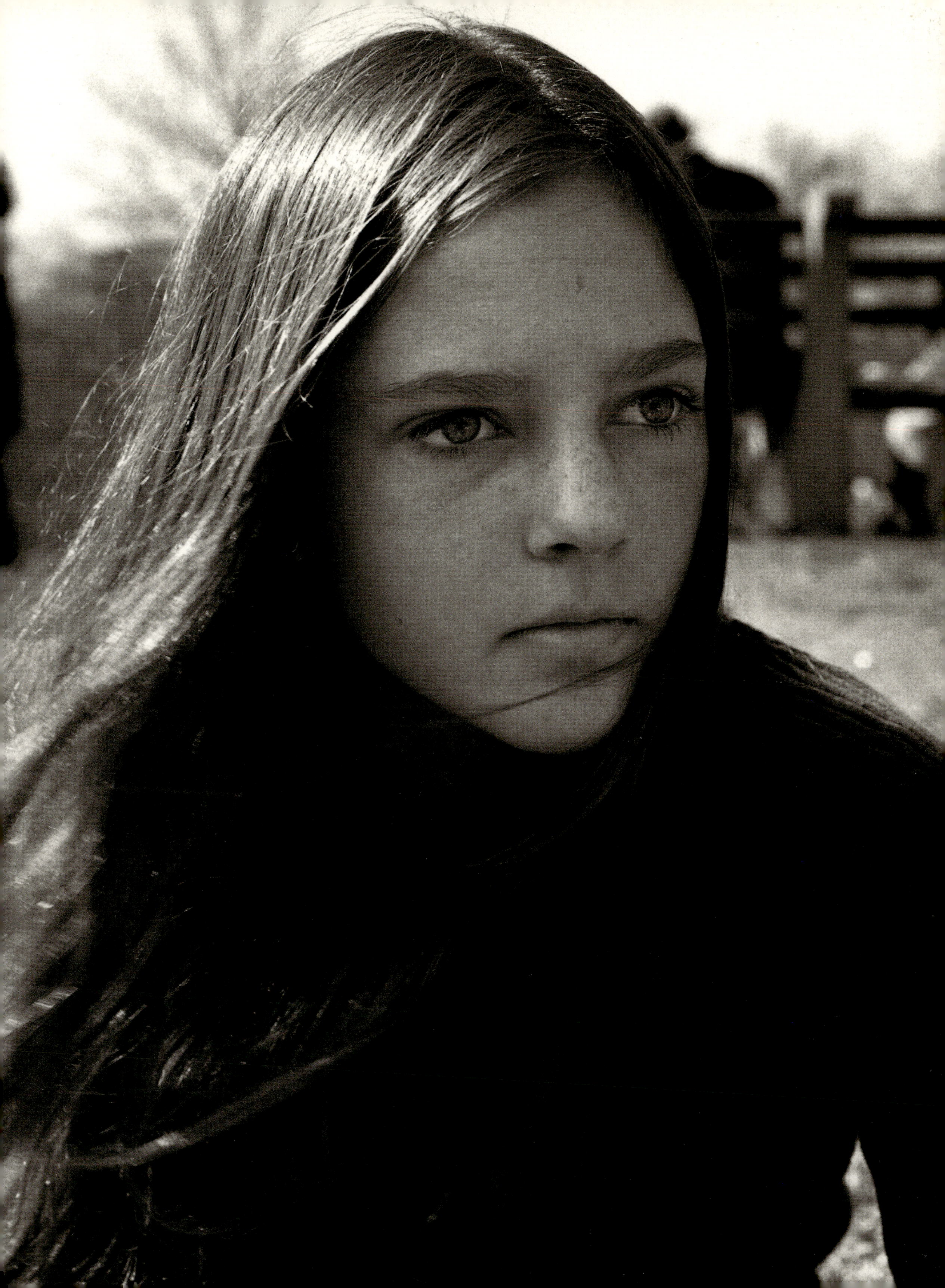

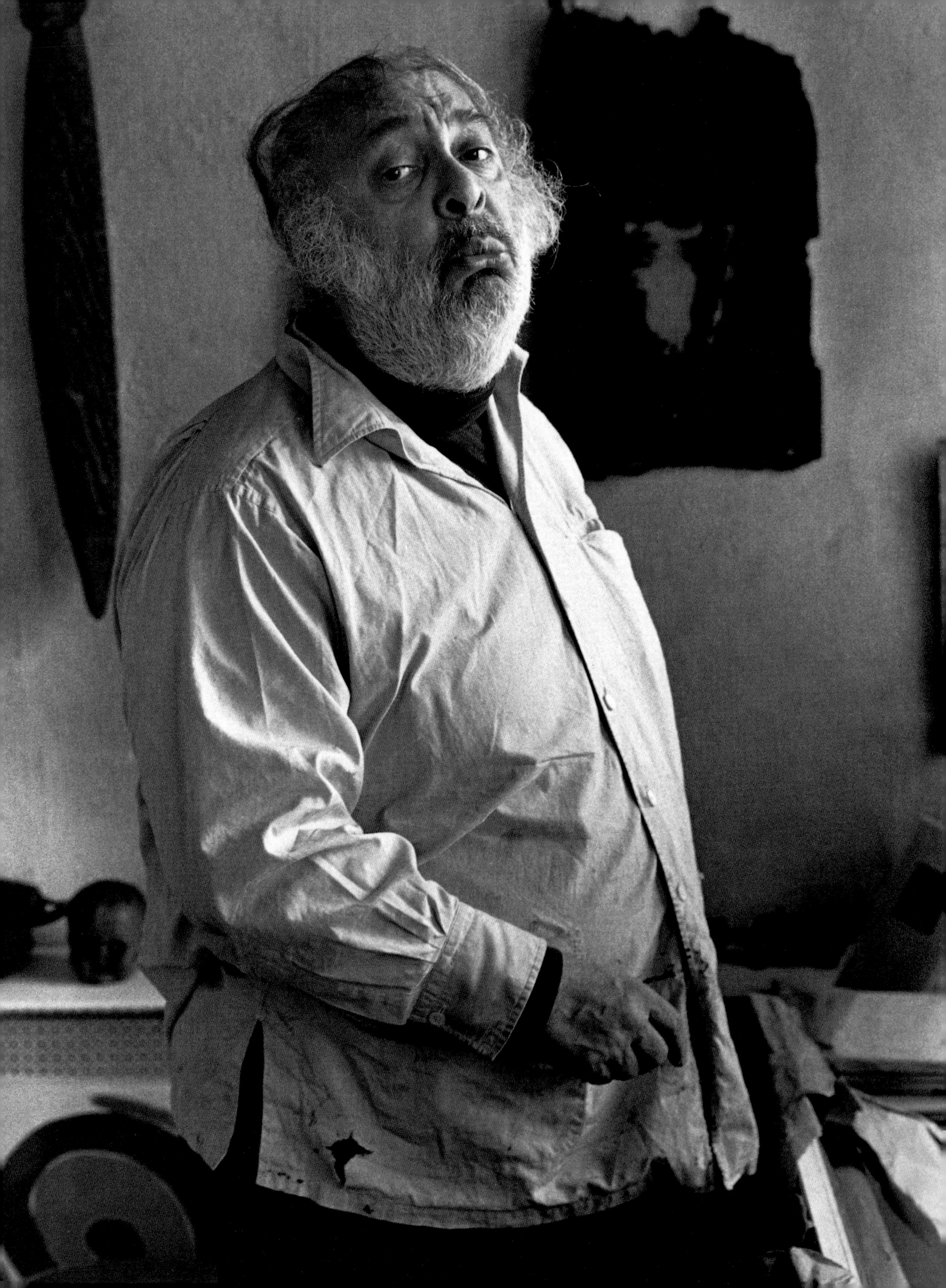

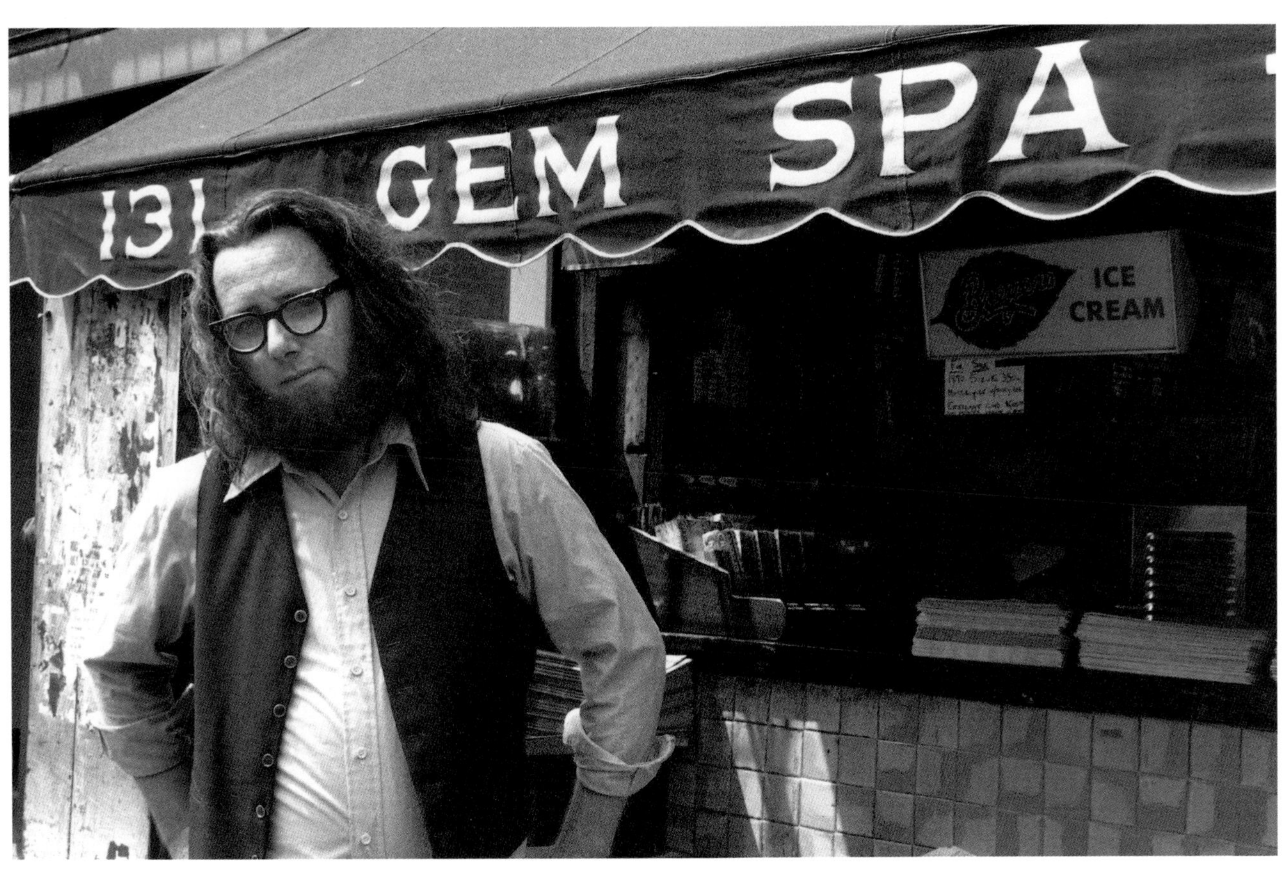
131 GEM SPA
ICE CREAM

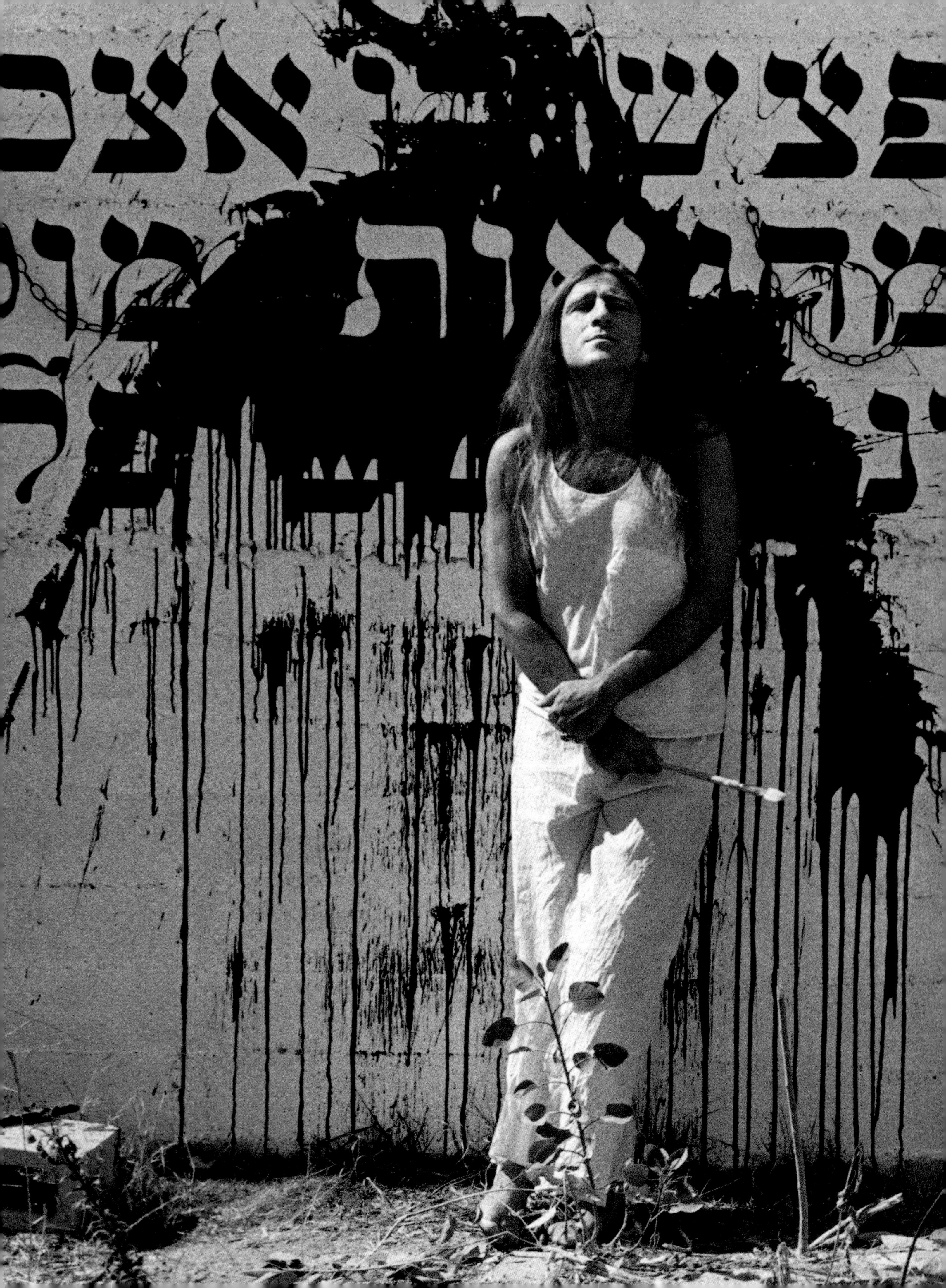

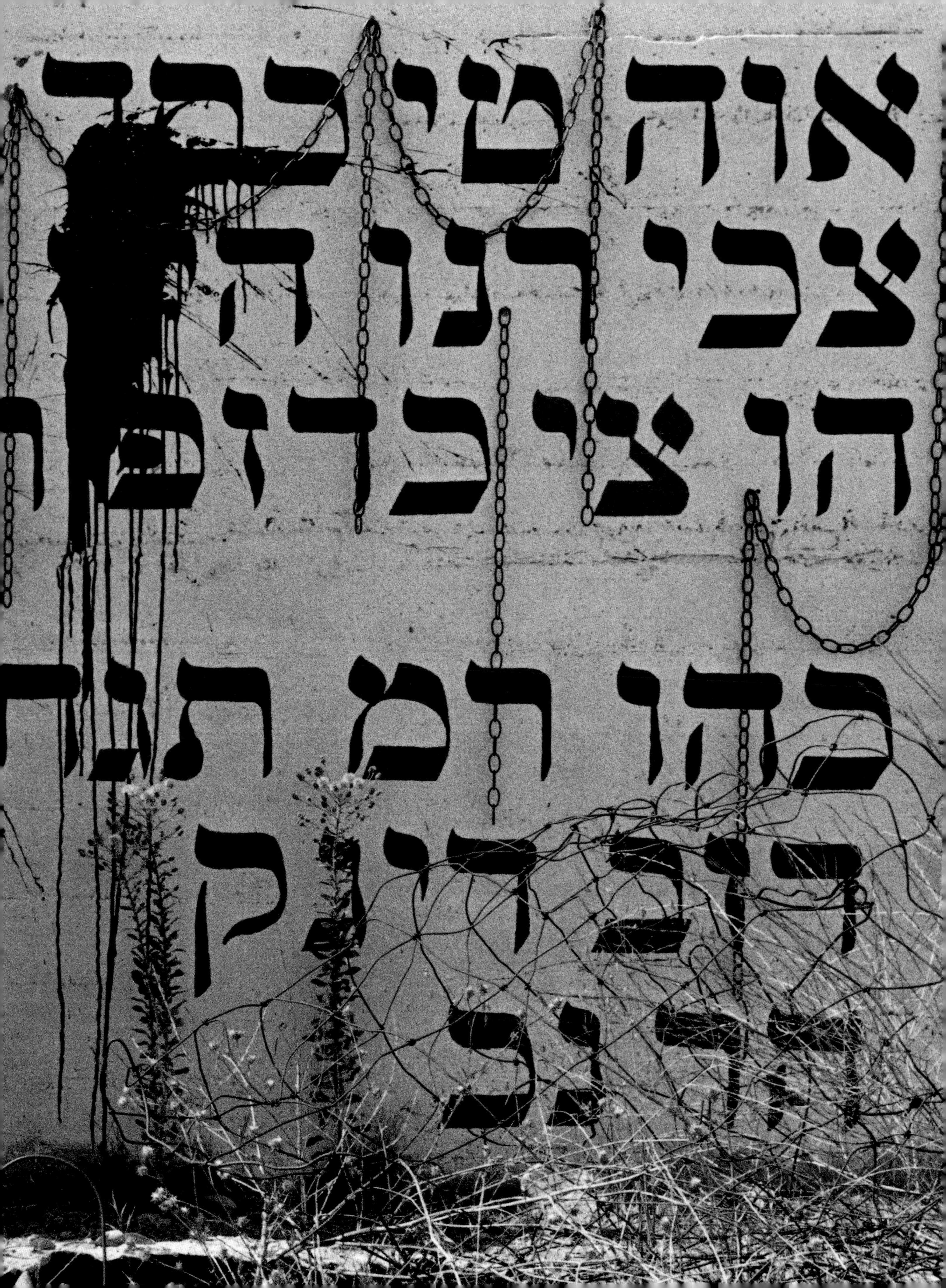

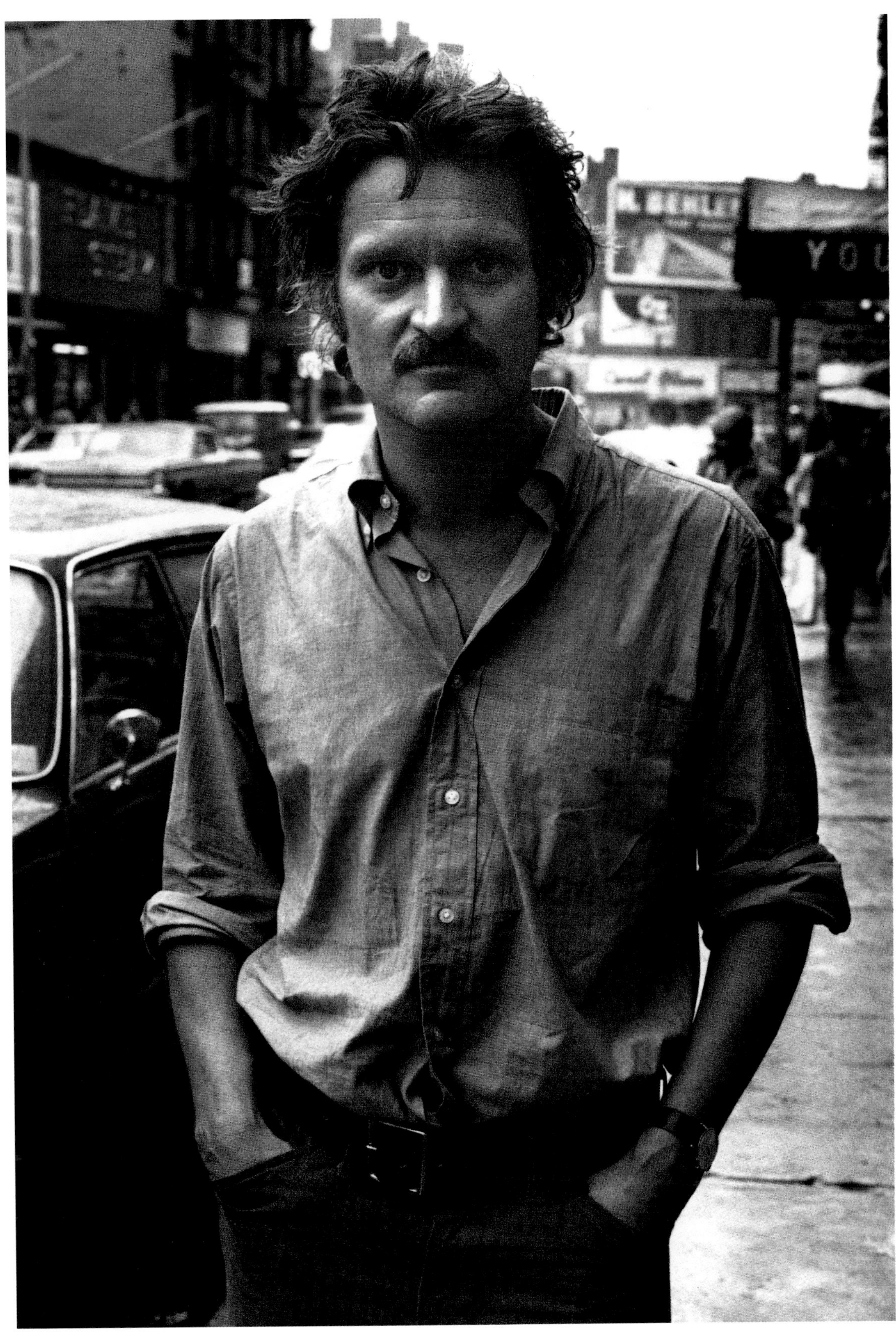
YOU

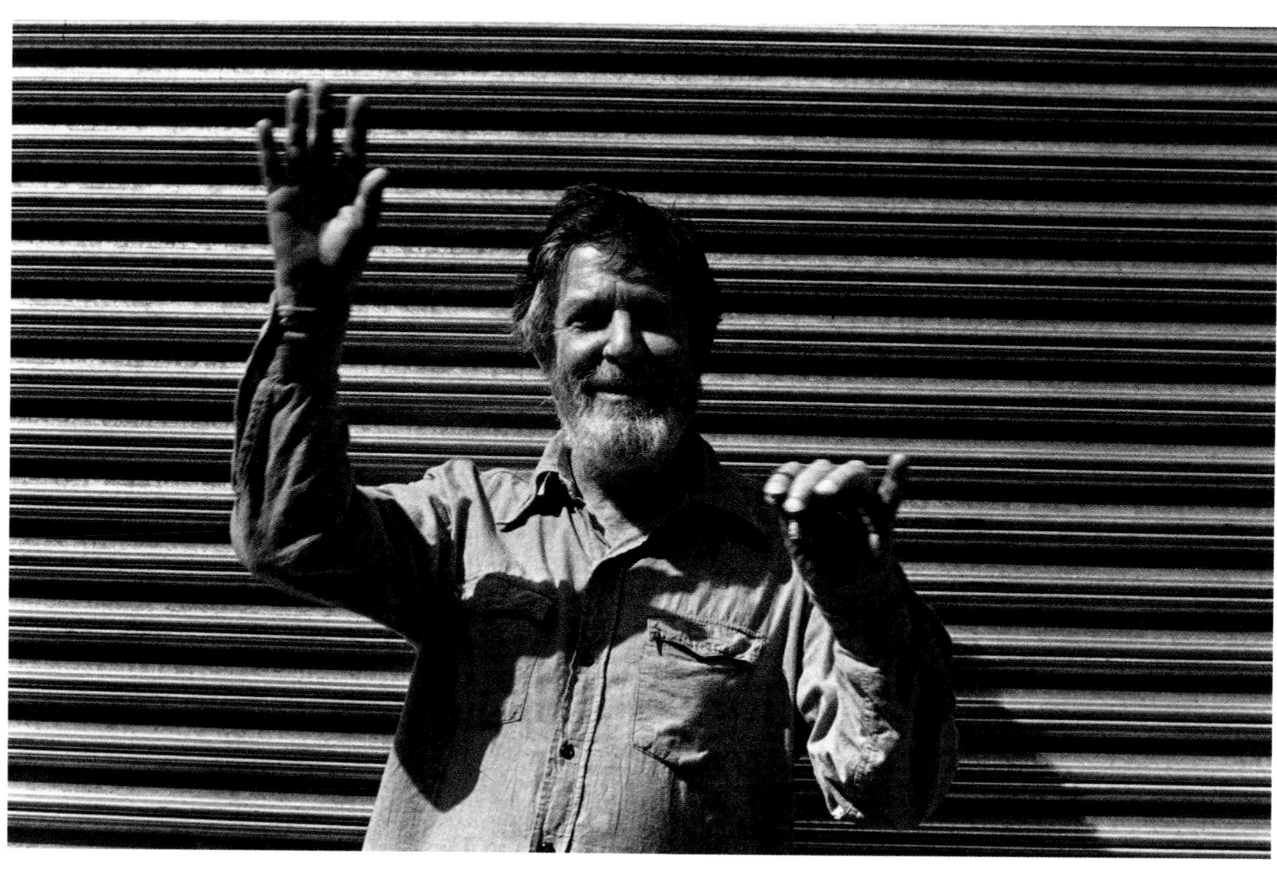

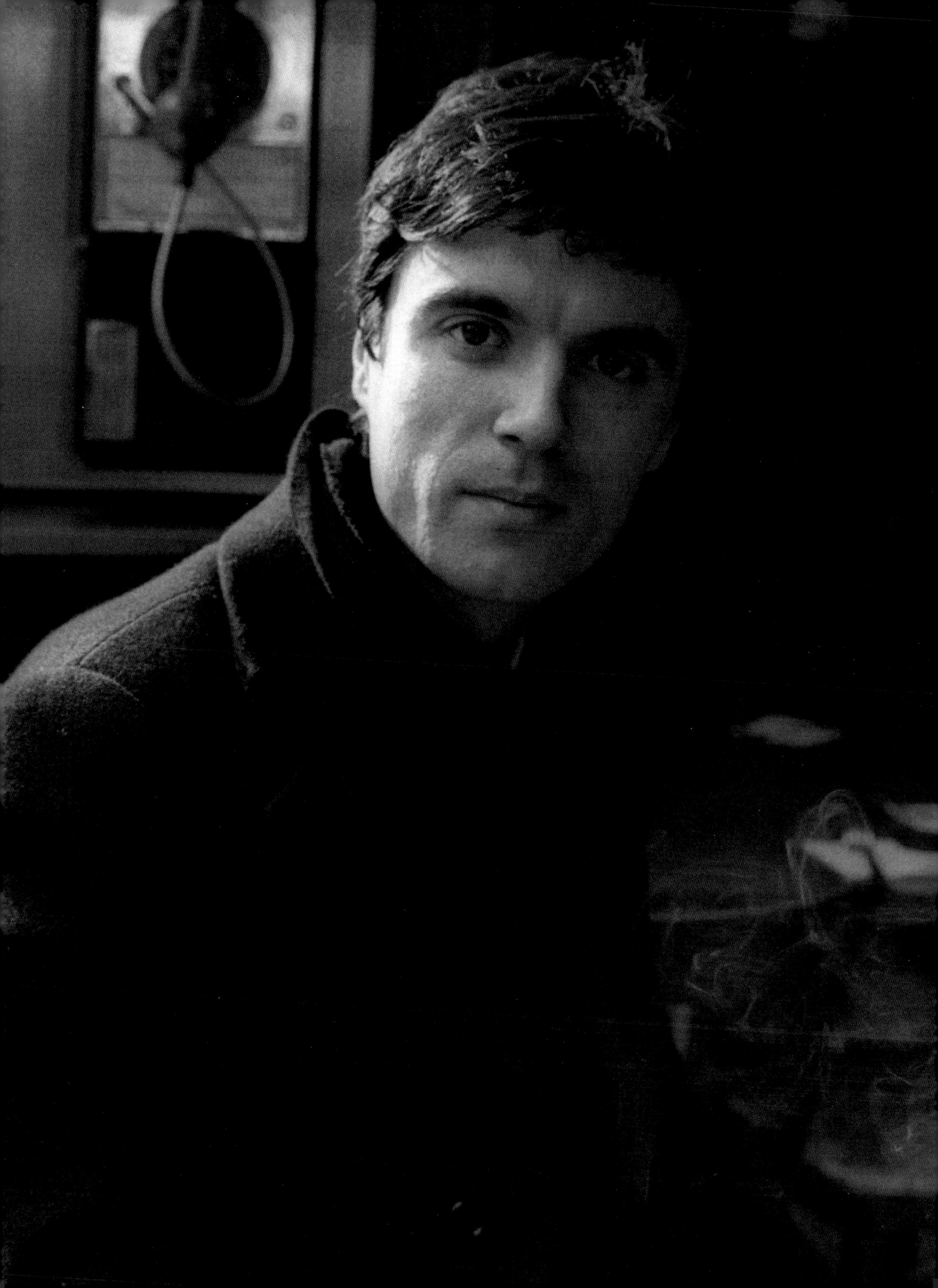

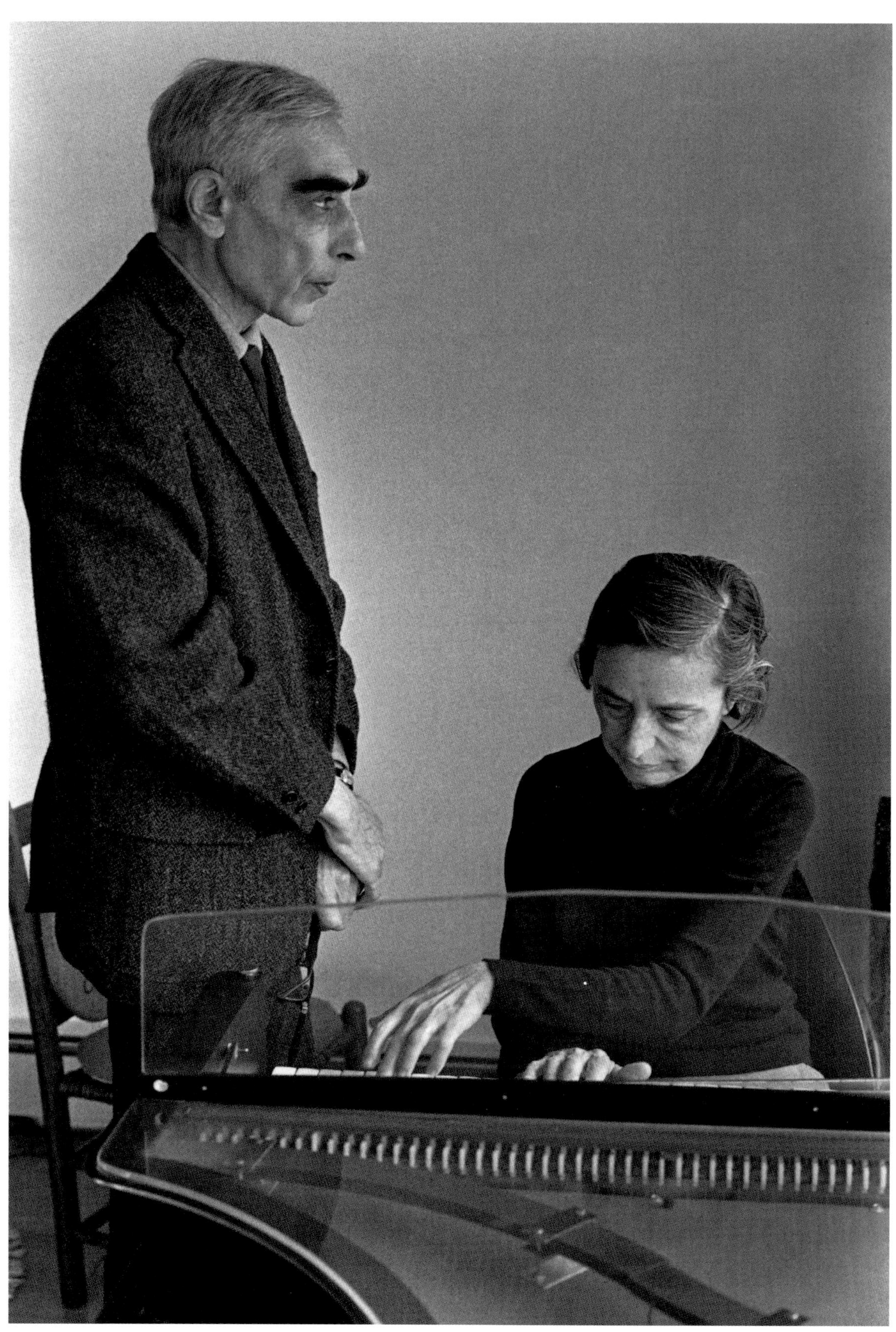

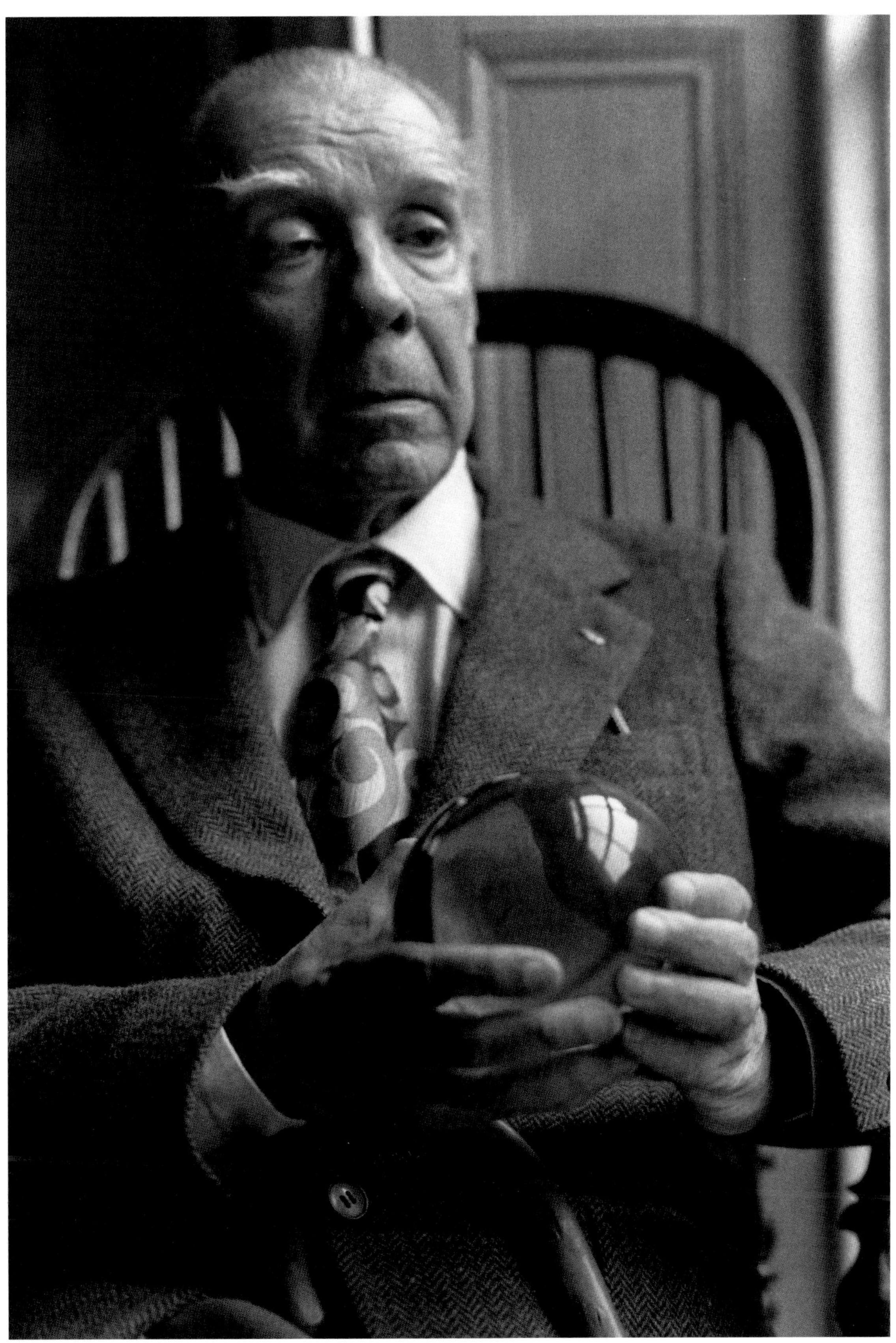

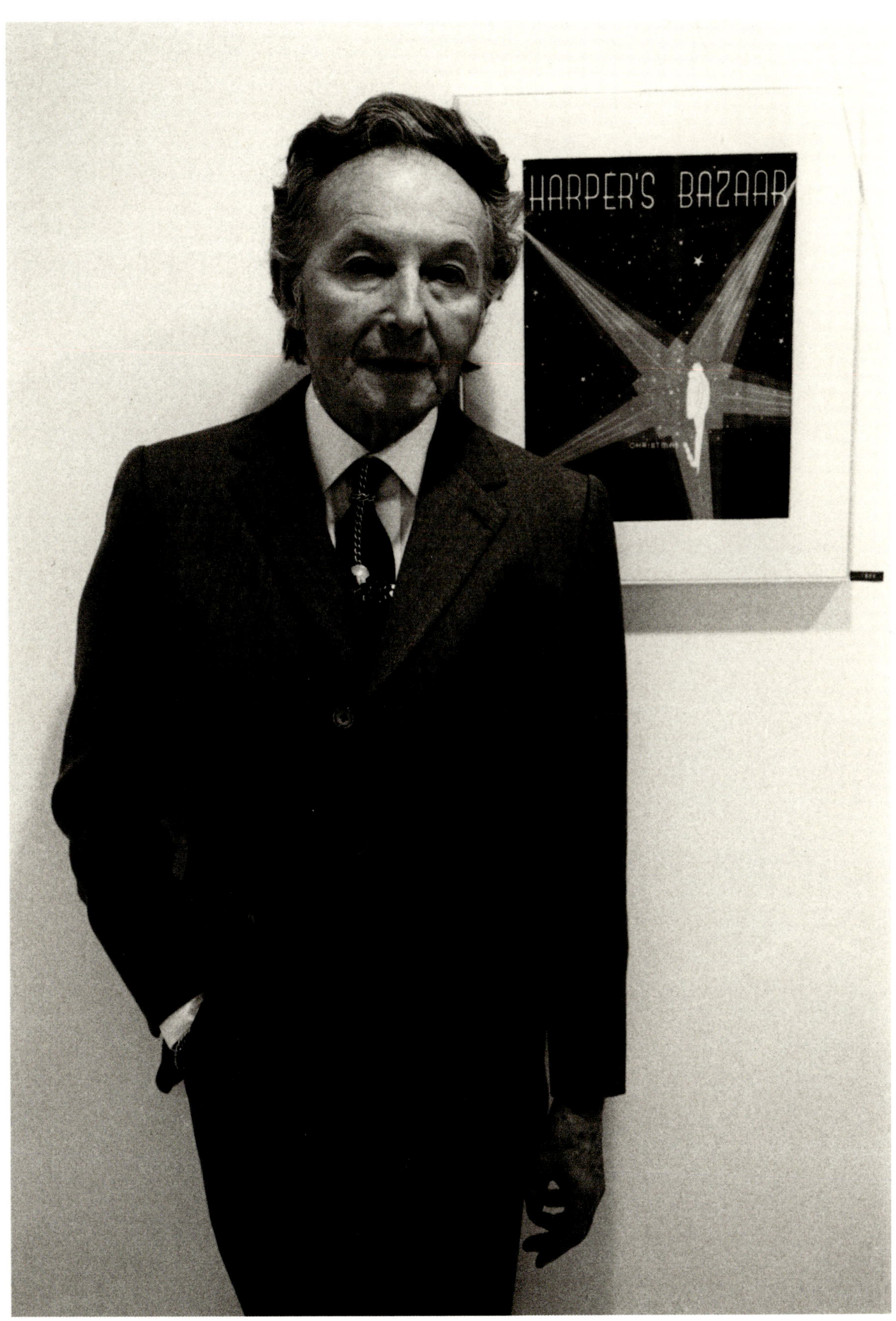
HARPER'S BAZAAR

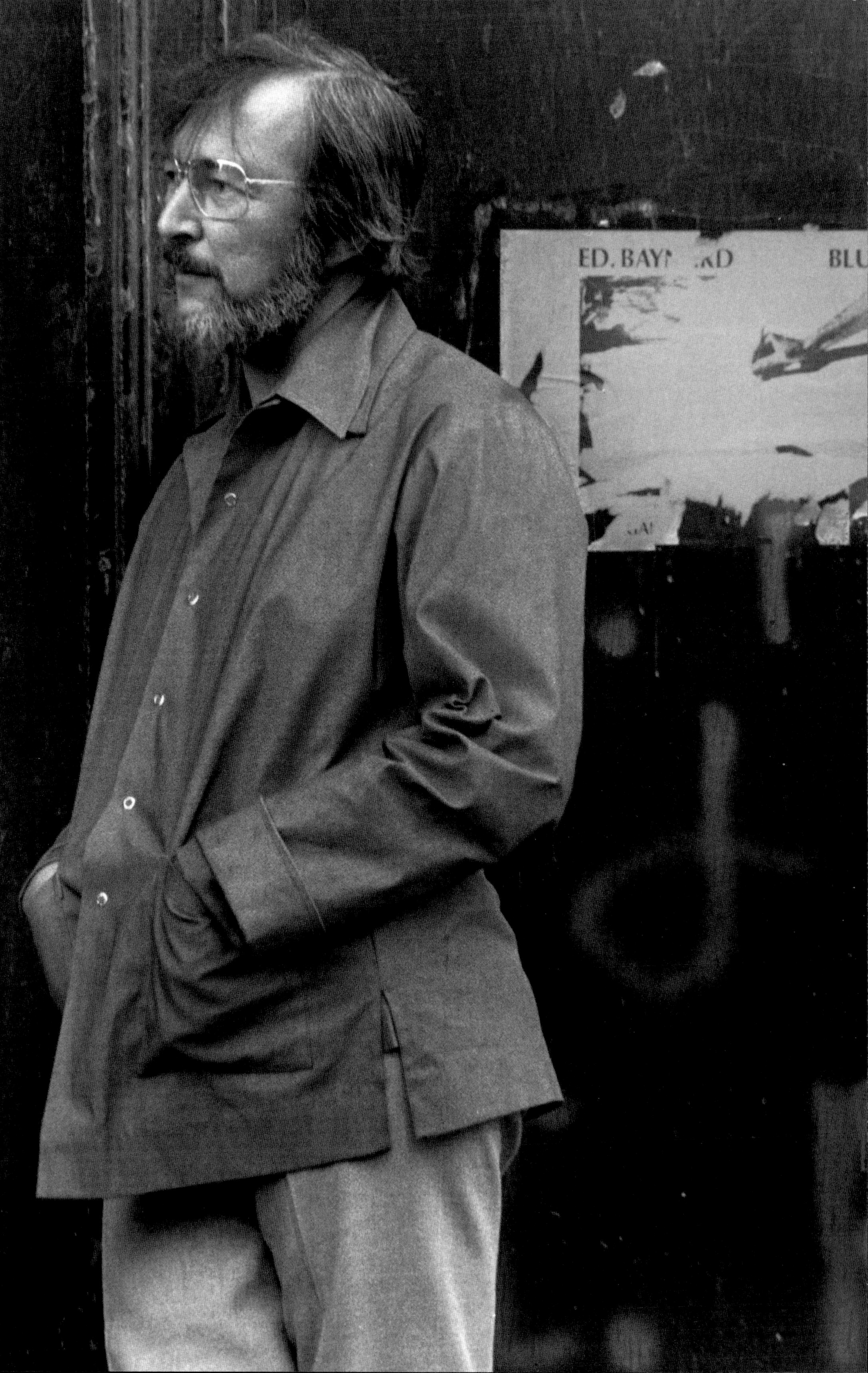
ED. BAYN RD
BLU

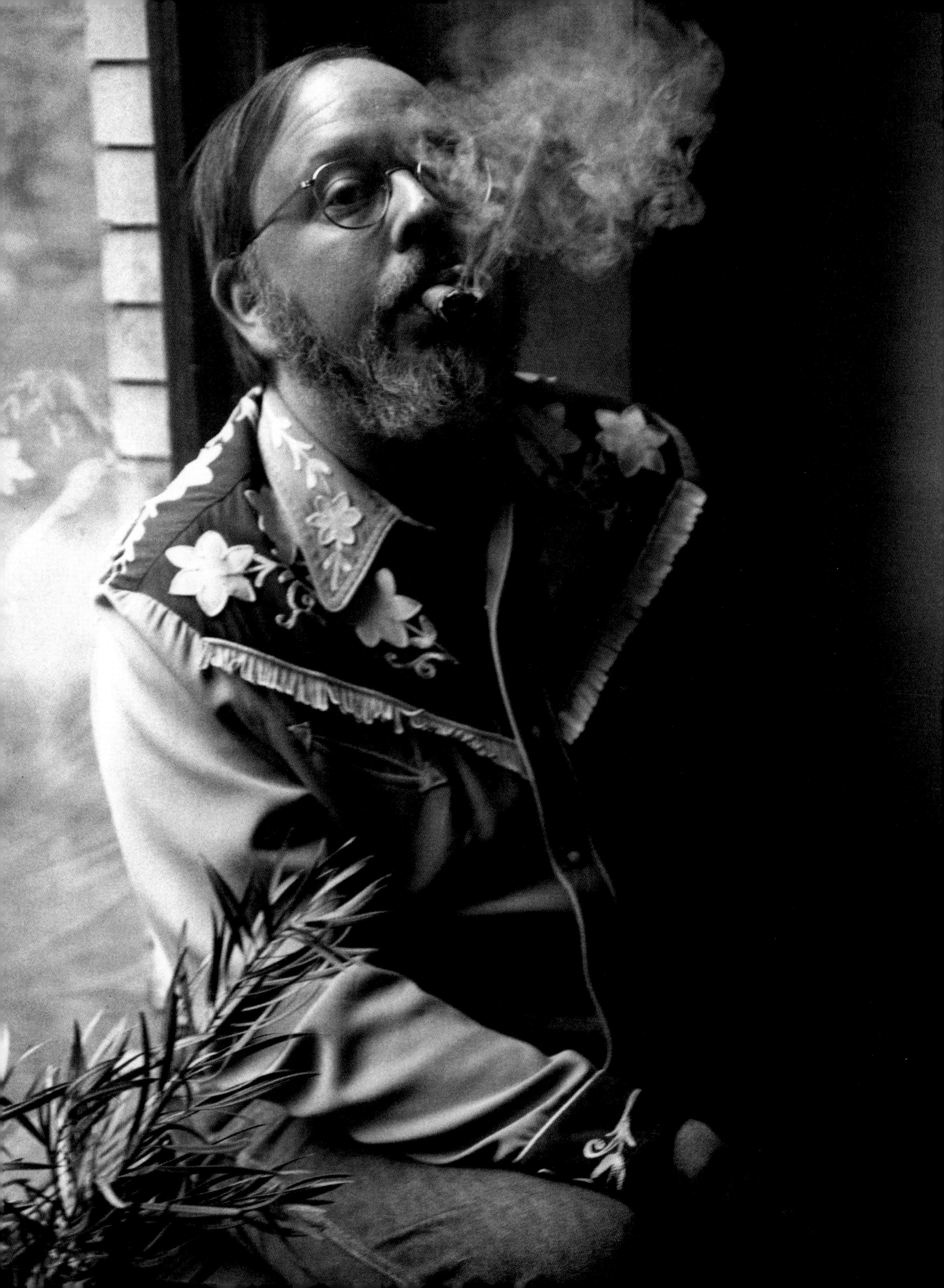

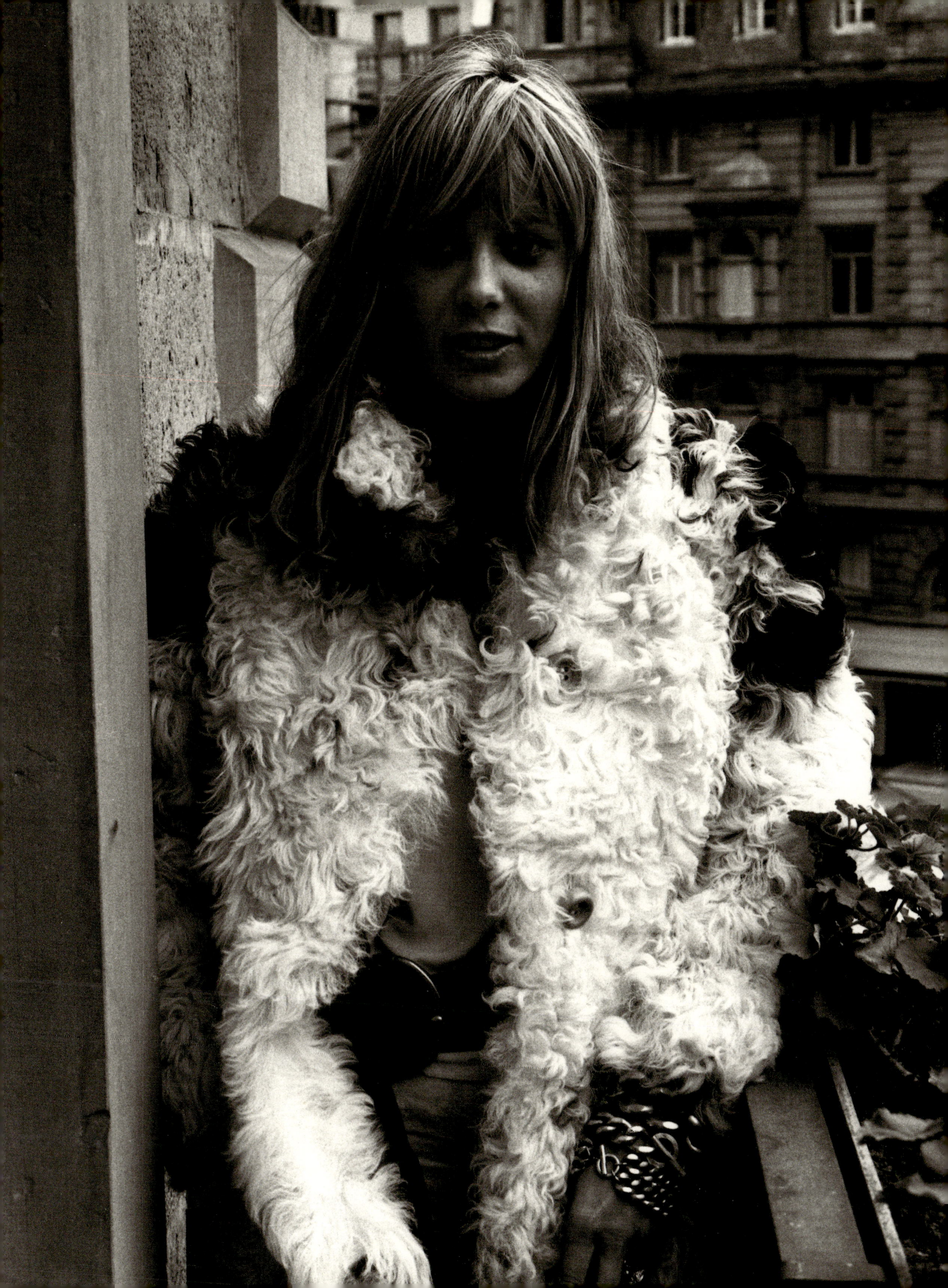

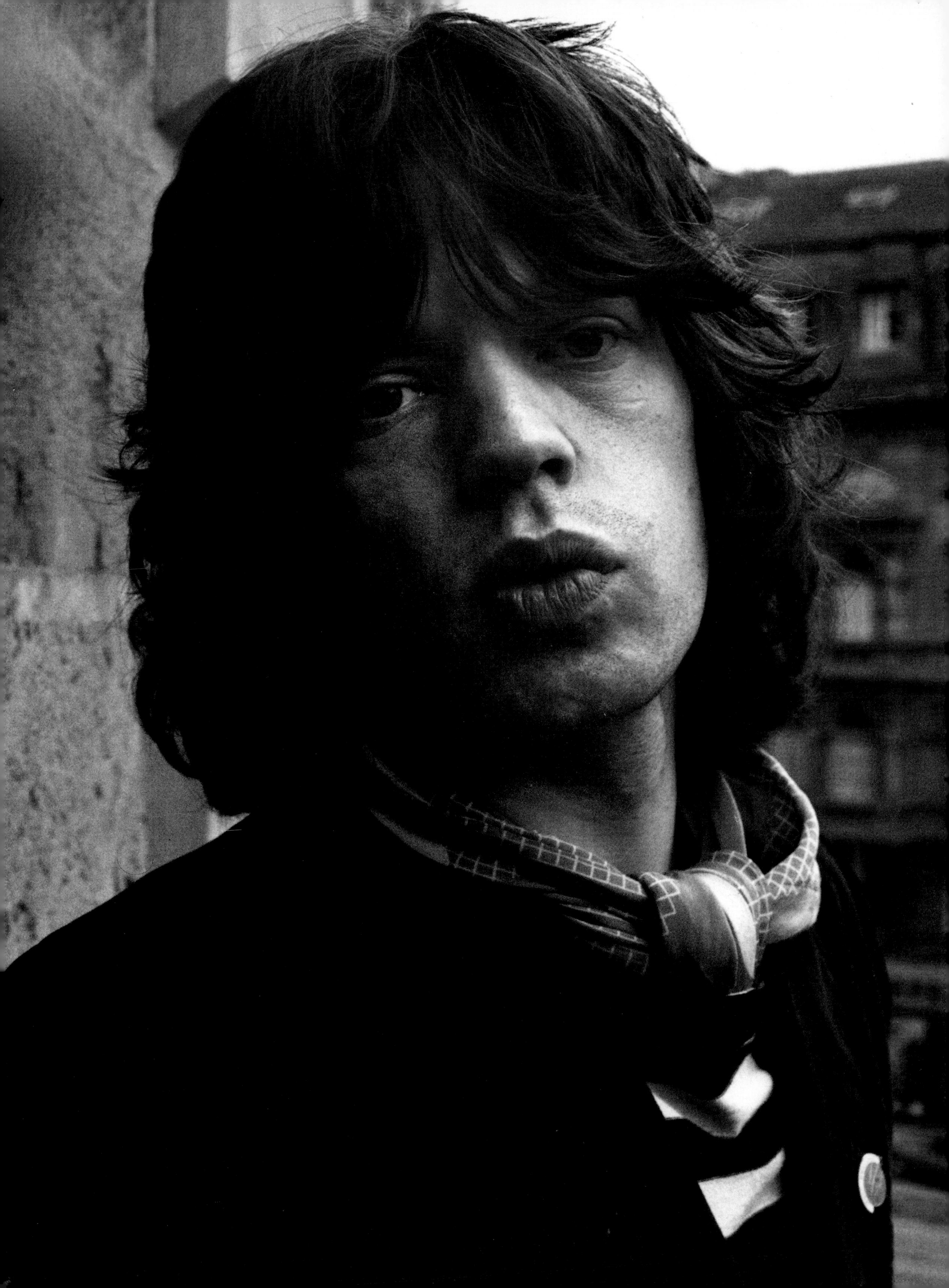

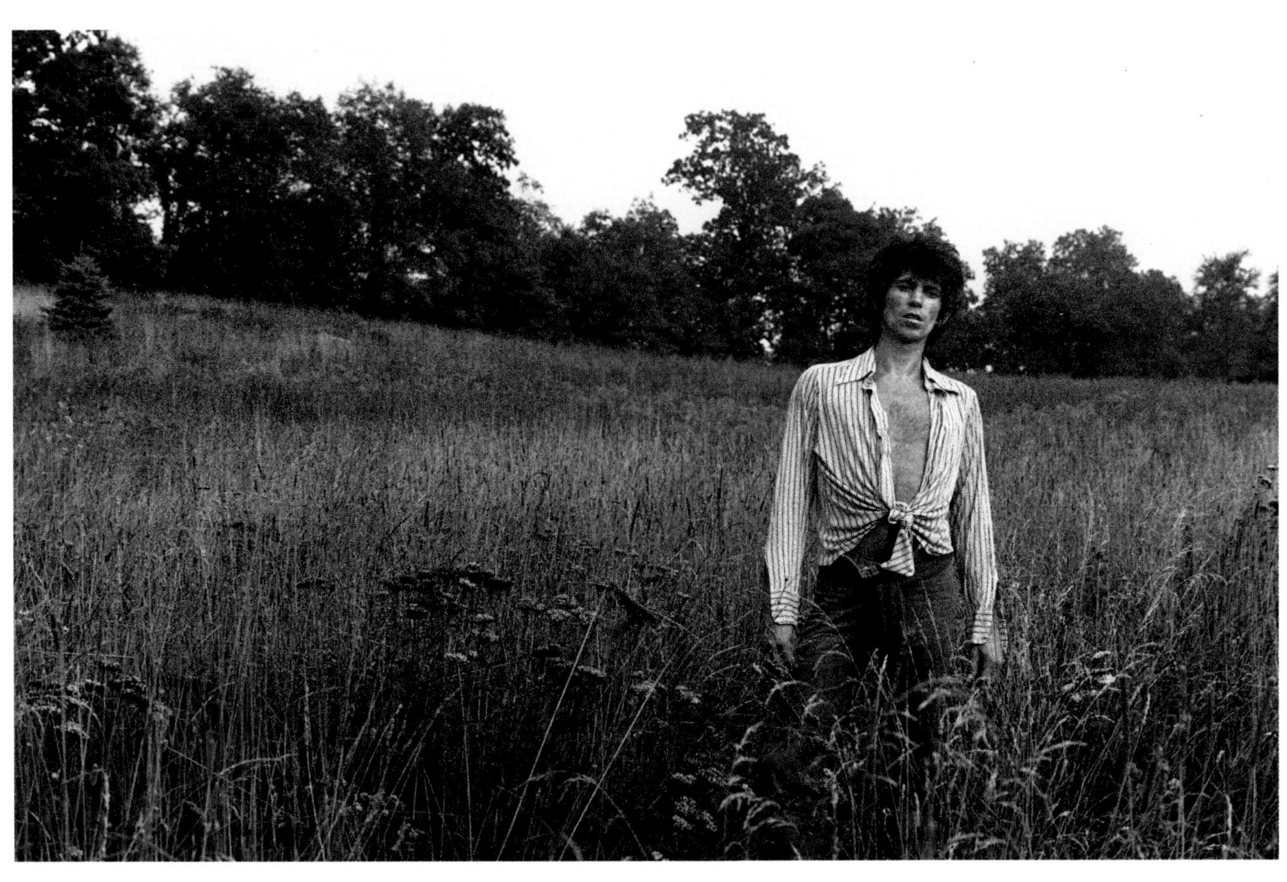

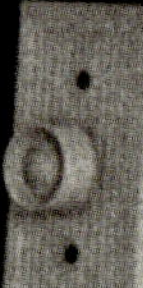
THE PARIS REVIEW

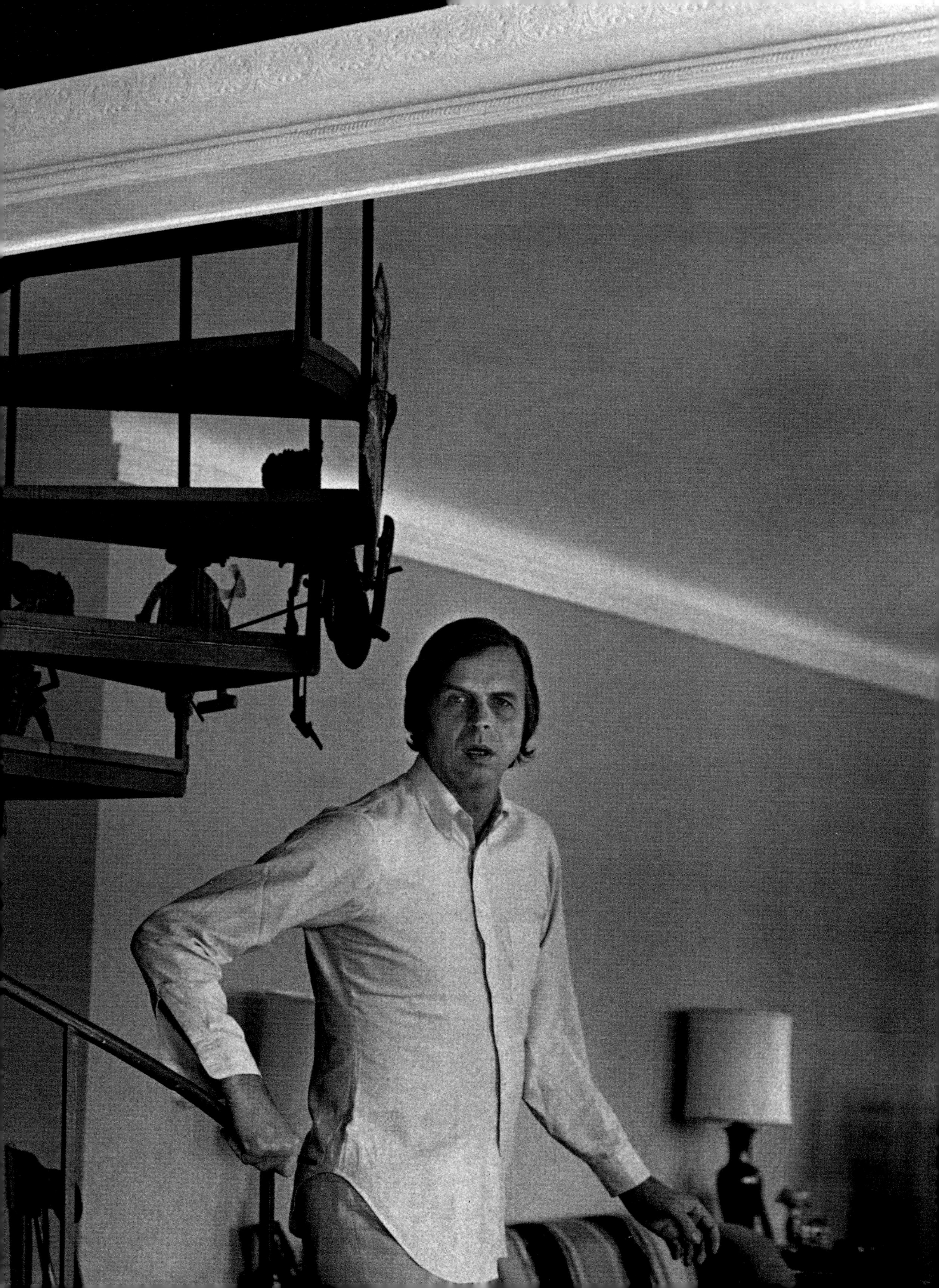

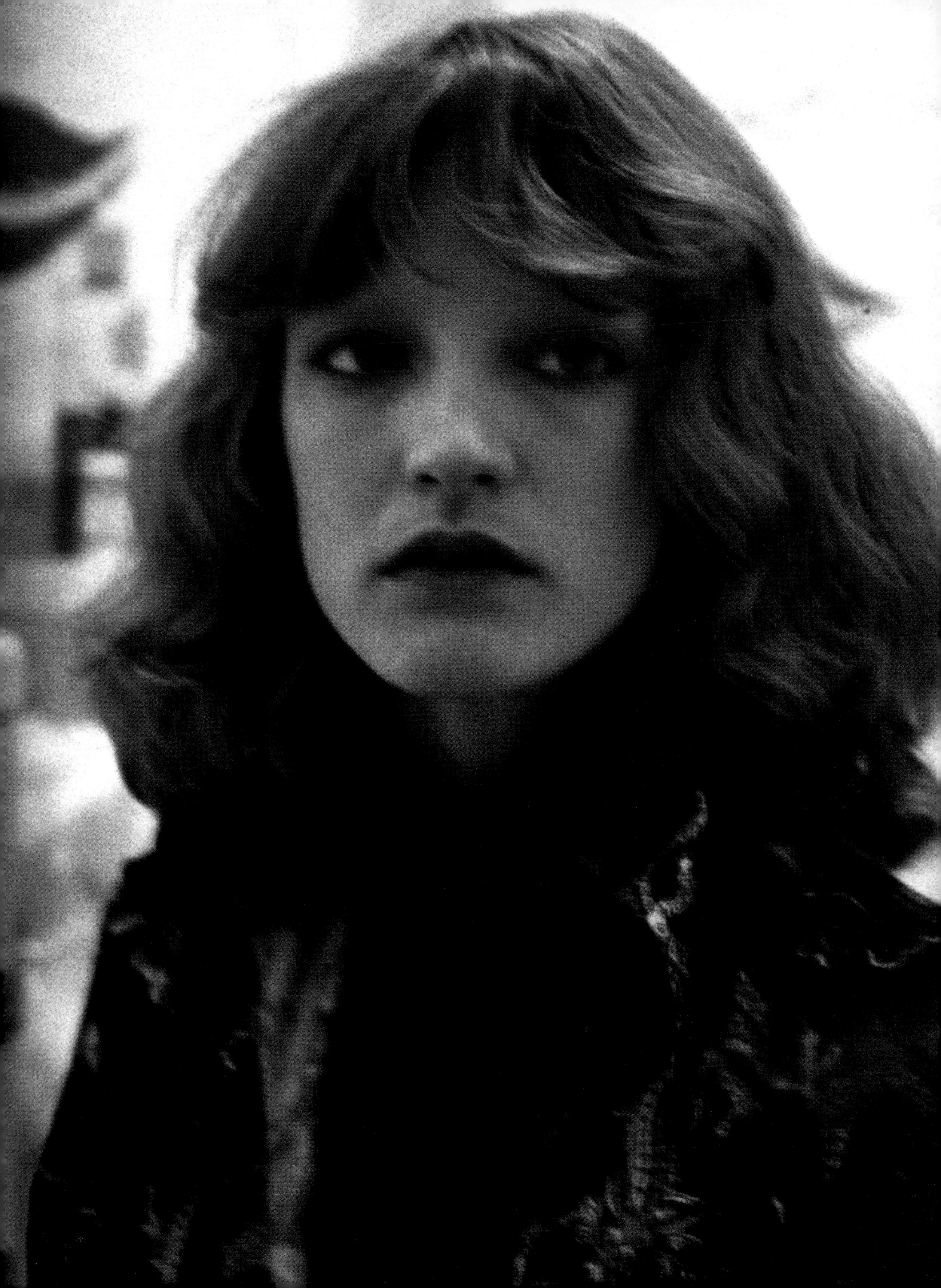

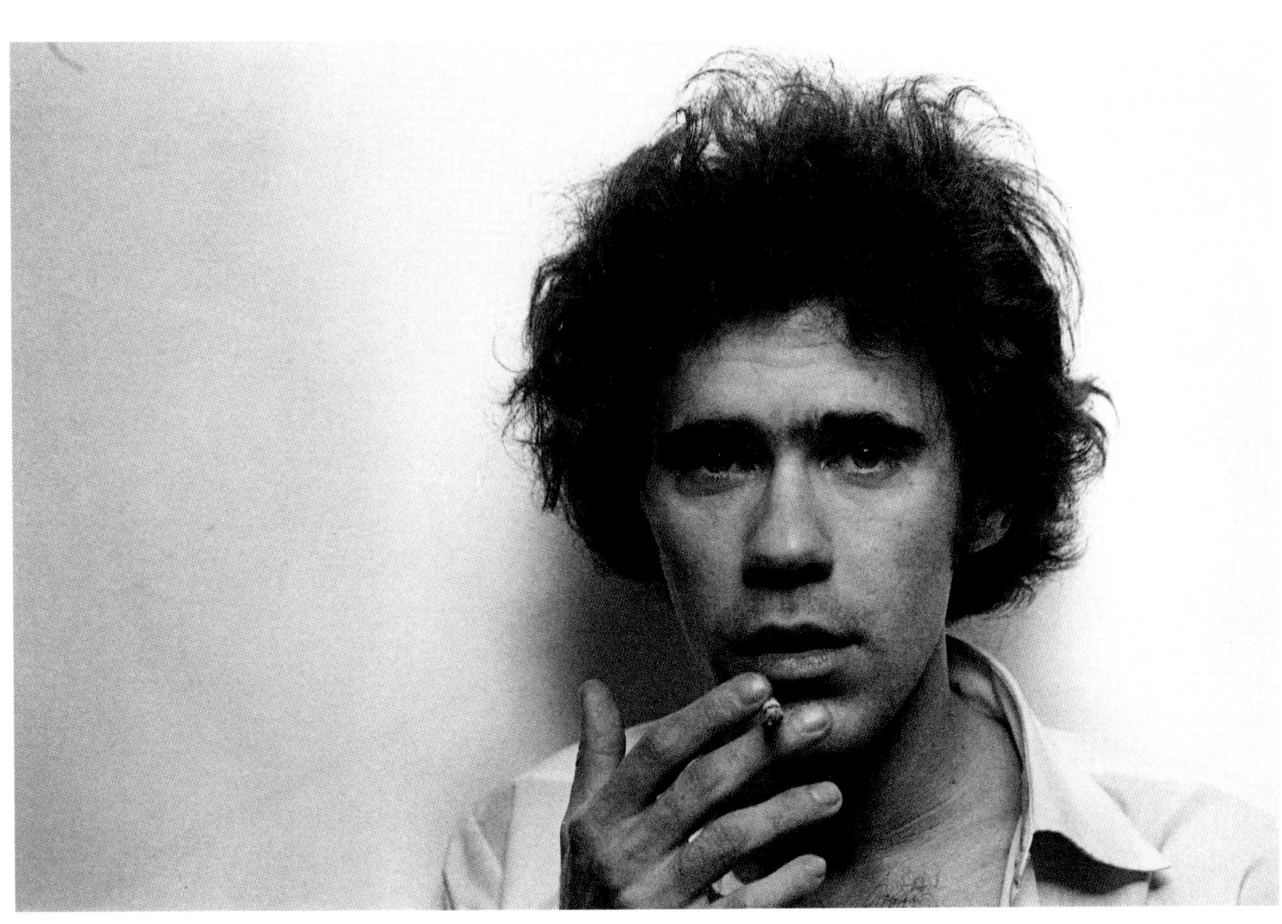

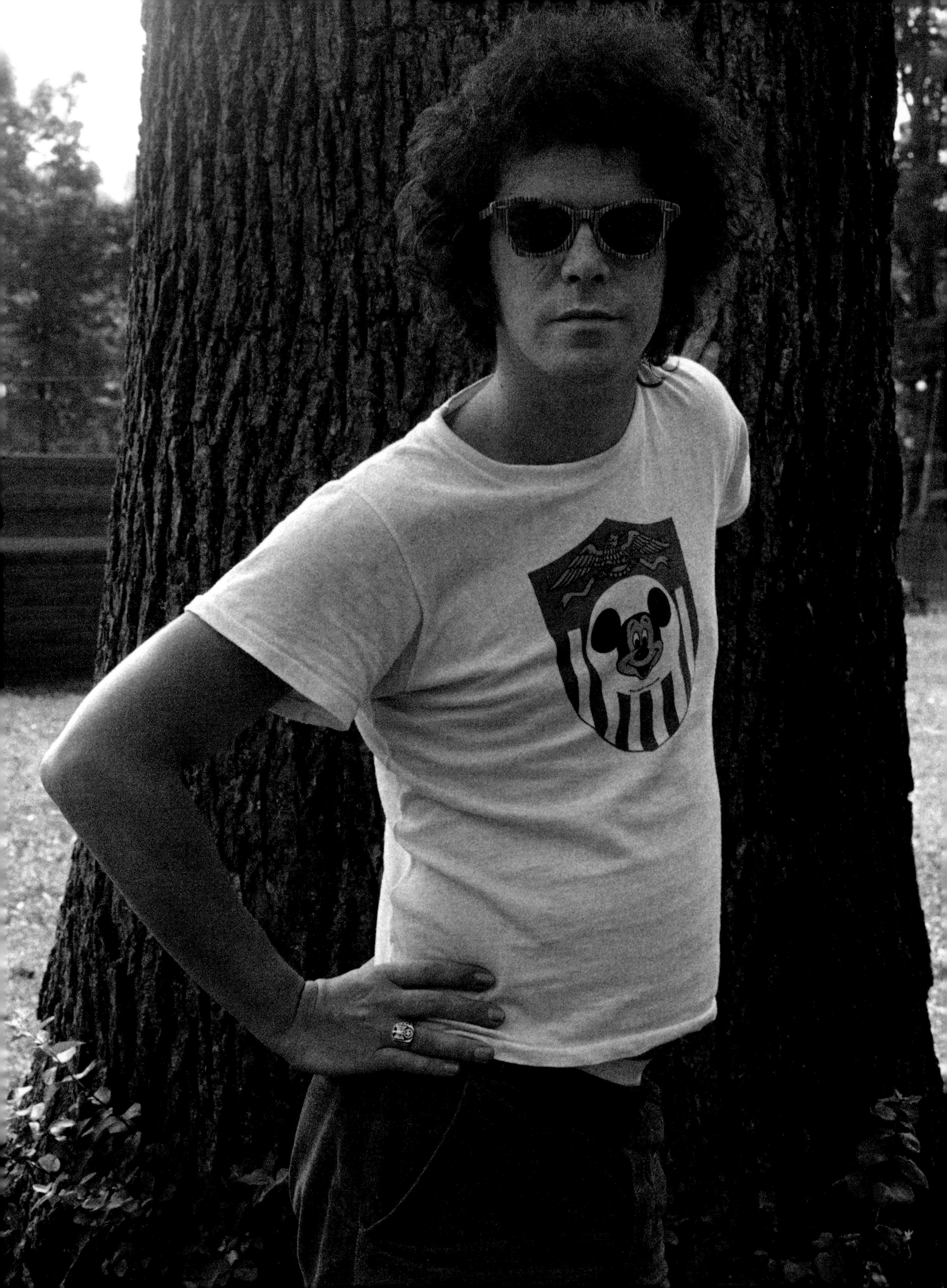

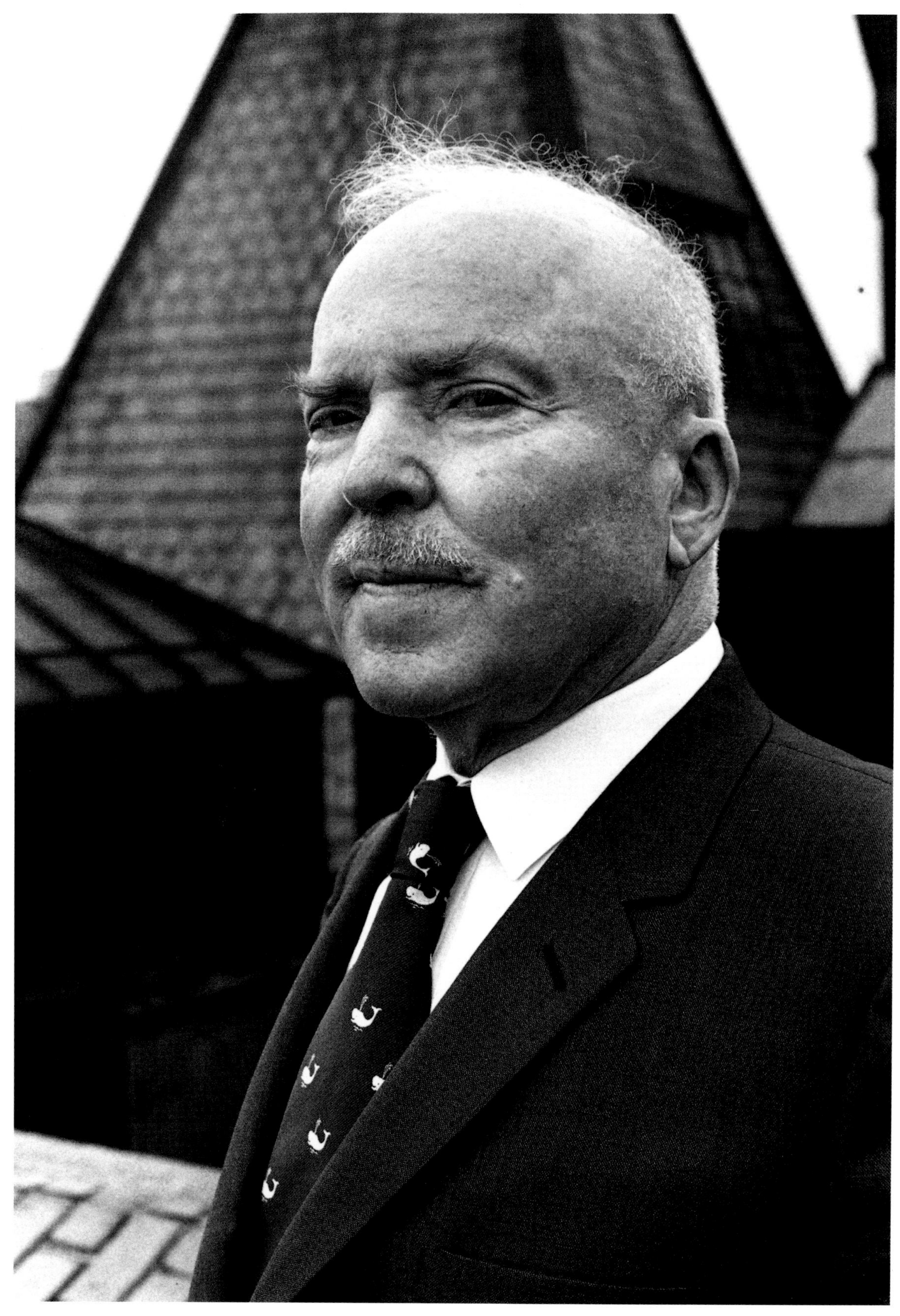

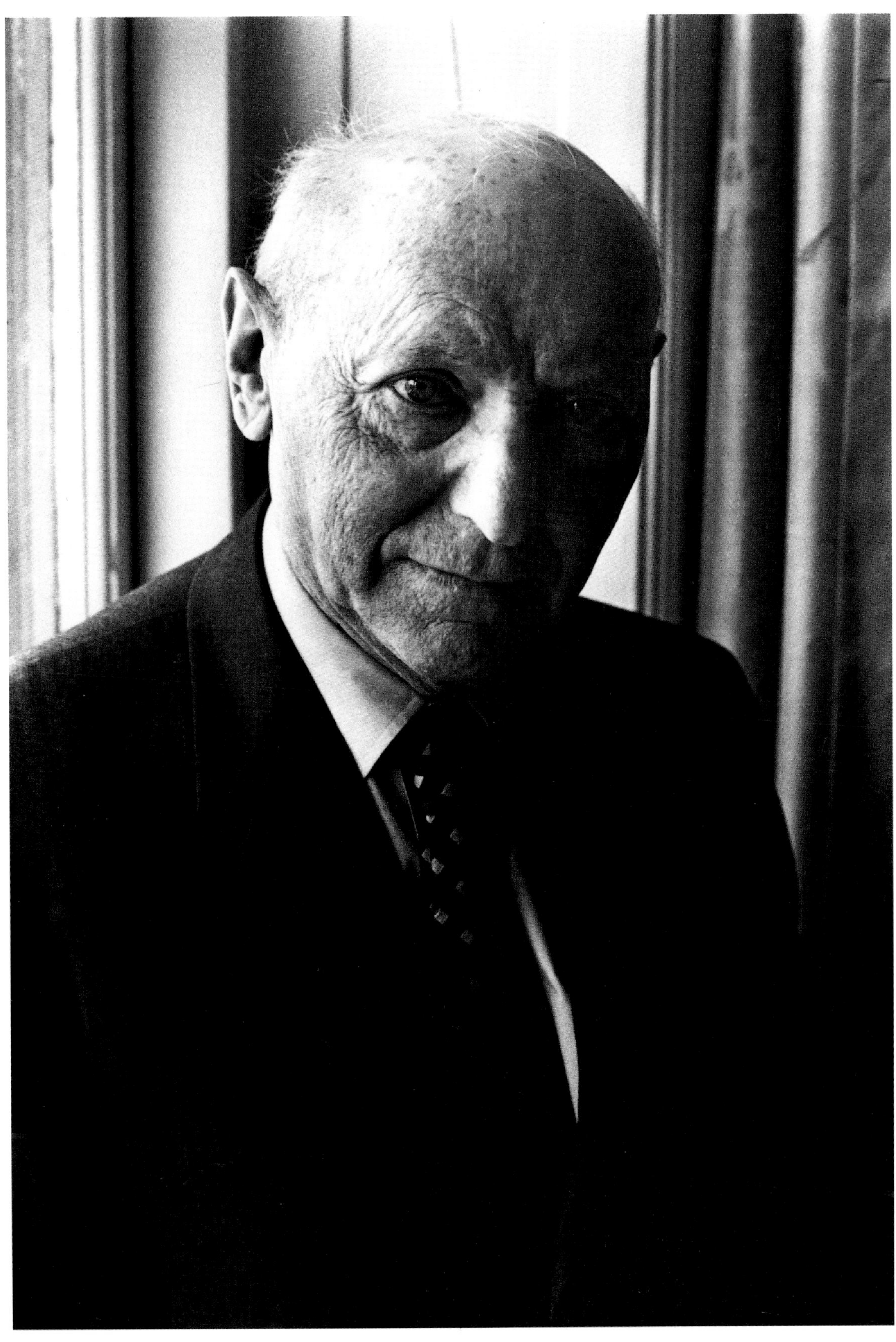

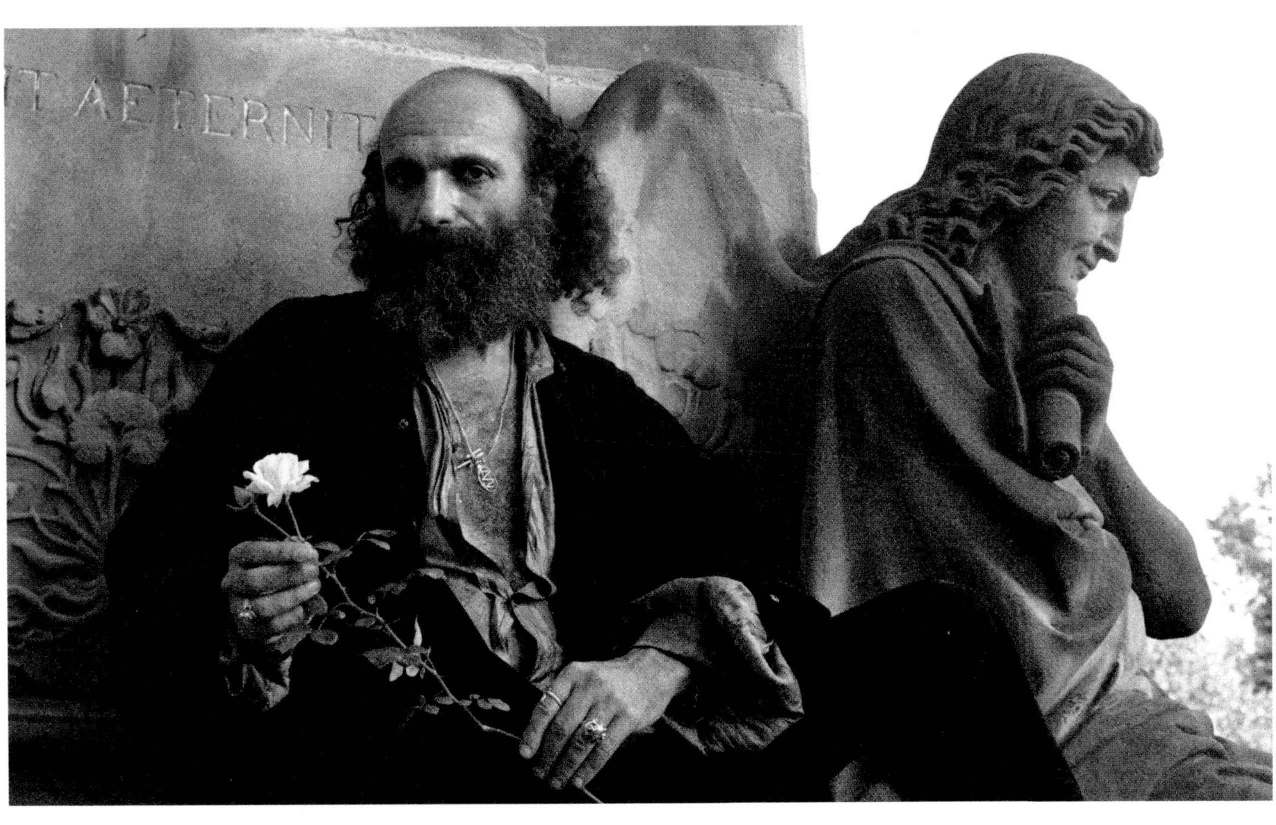
T AETERNIT

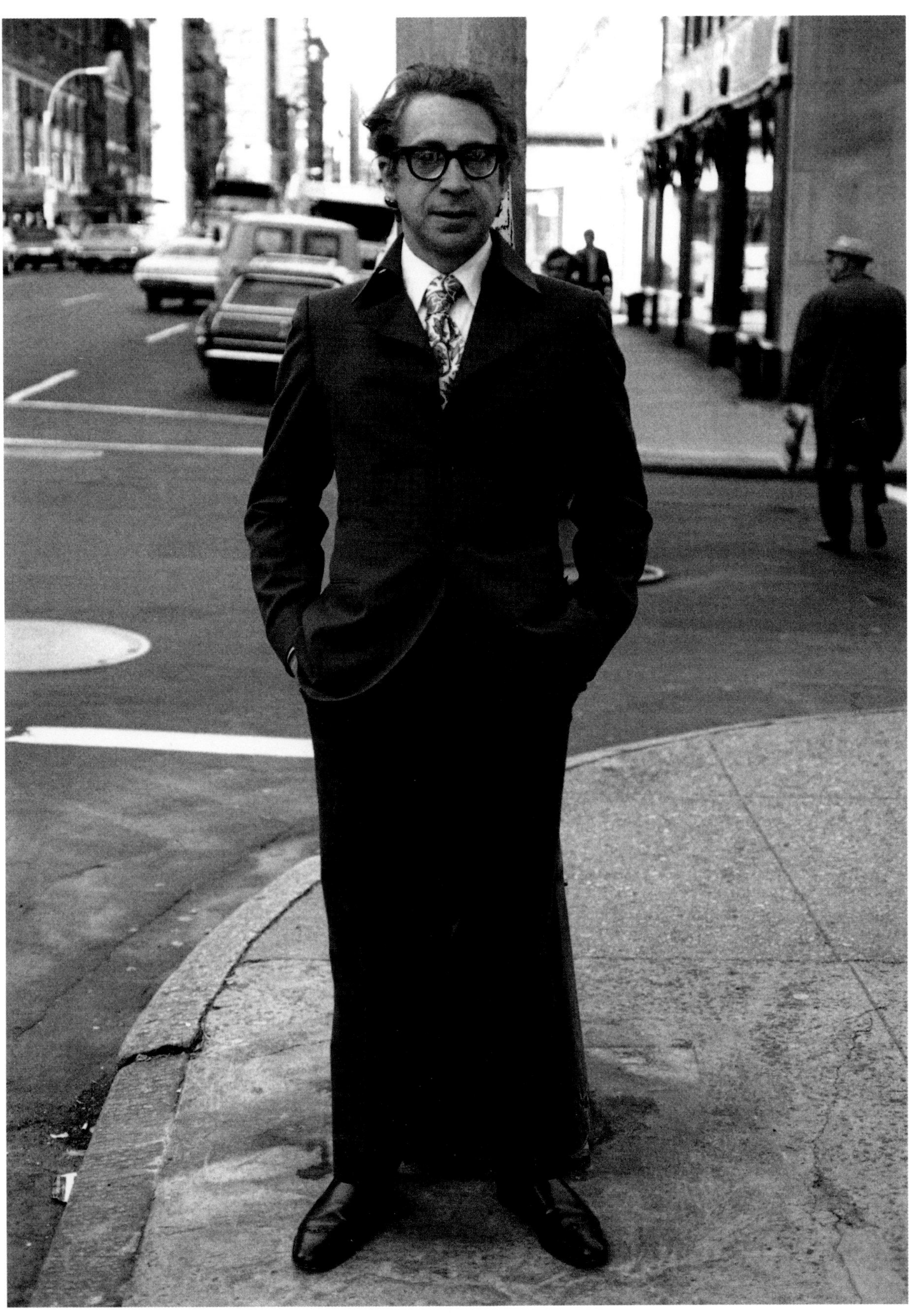

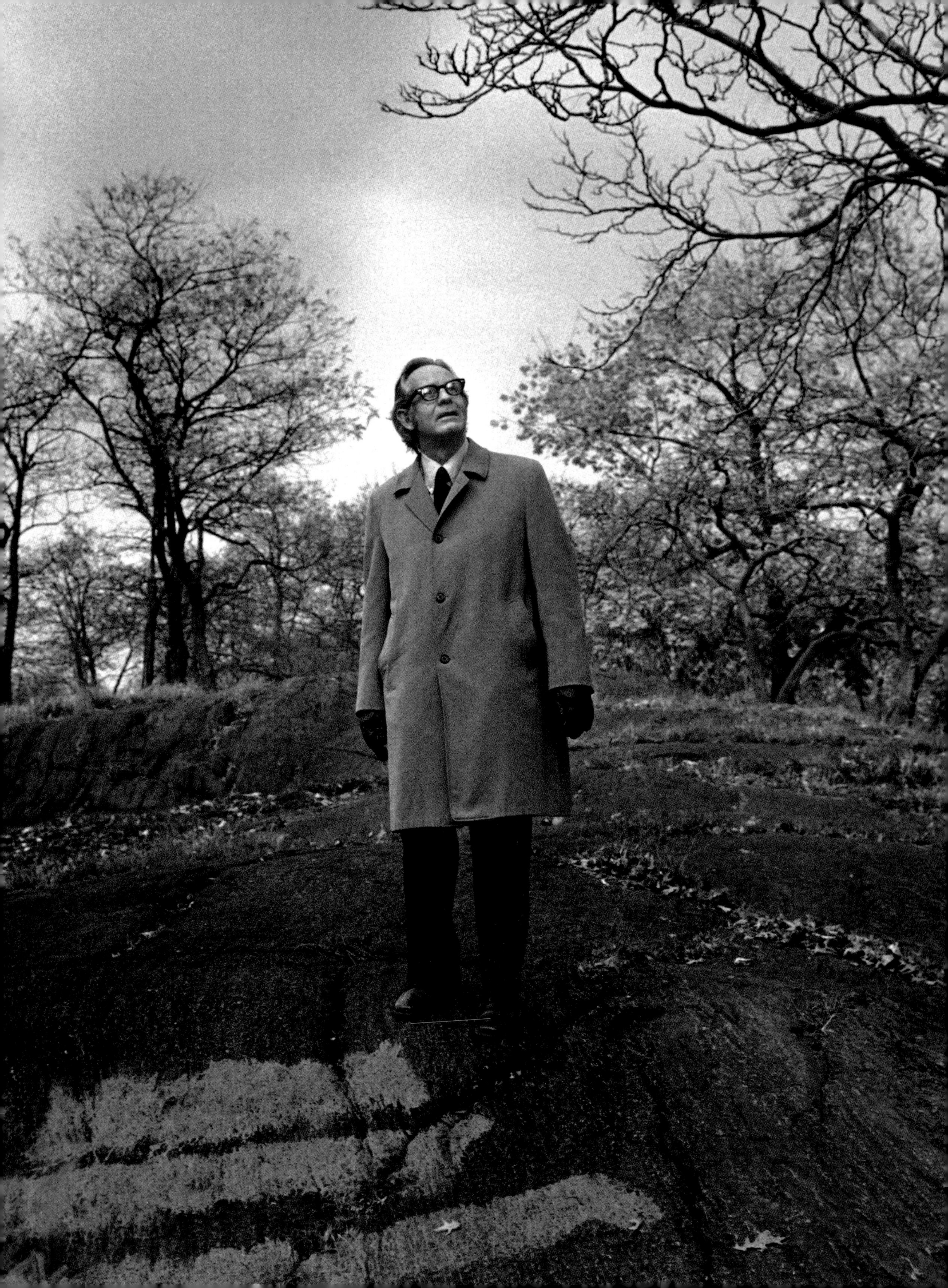

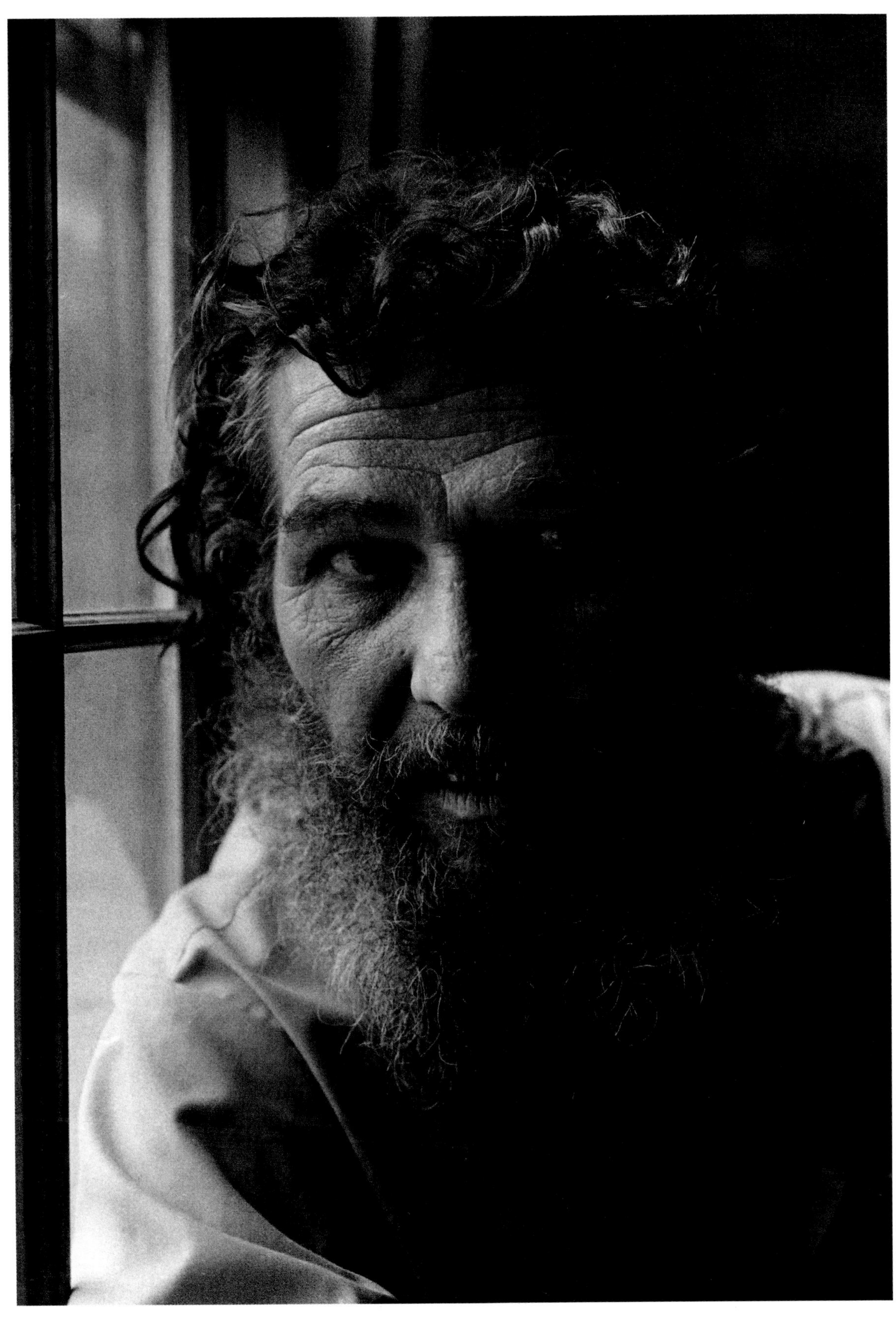

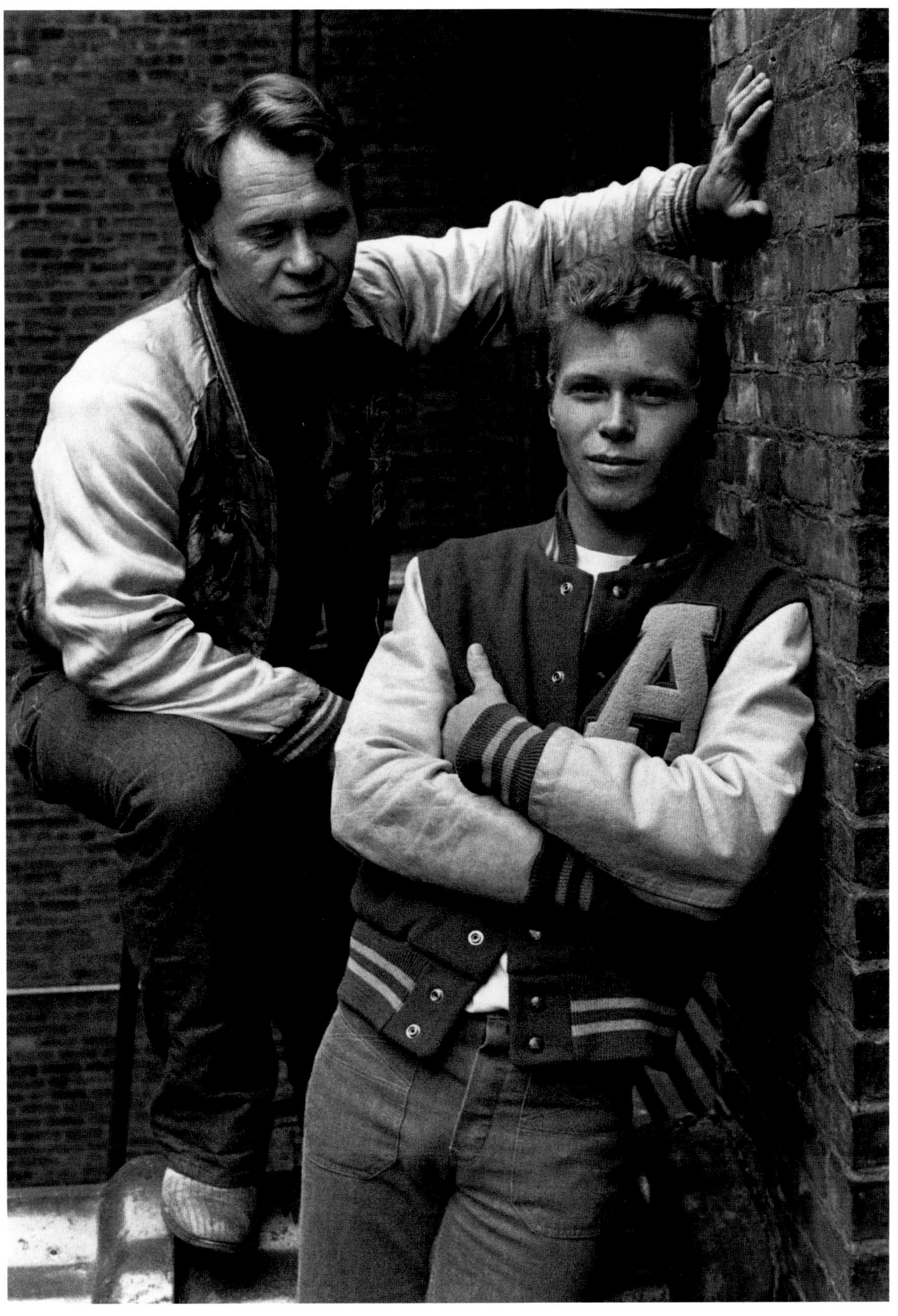

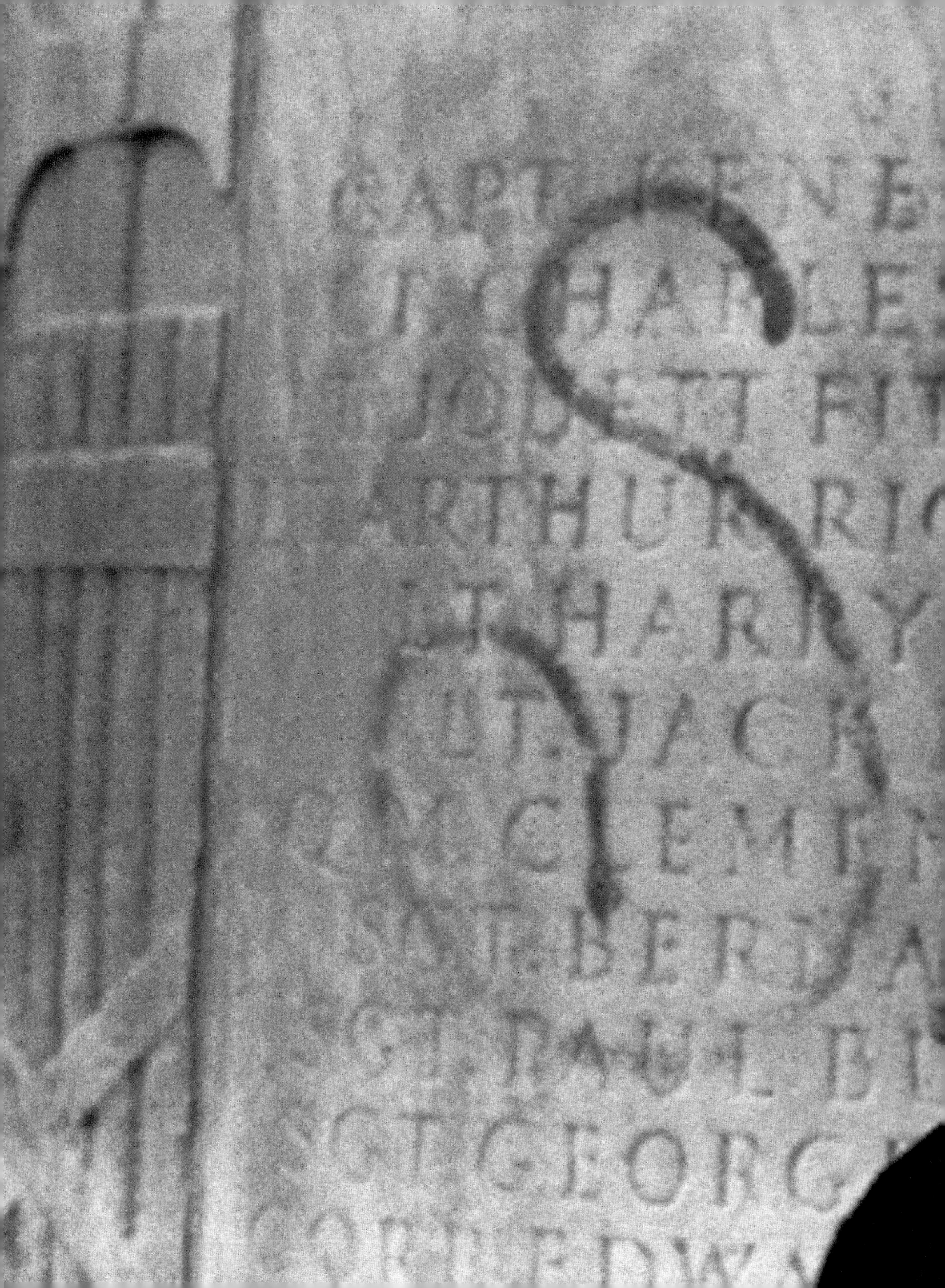
LT. ARTHUR
LT. HARRY
SGT. GEORG

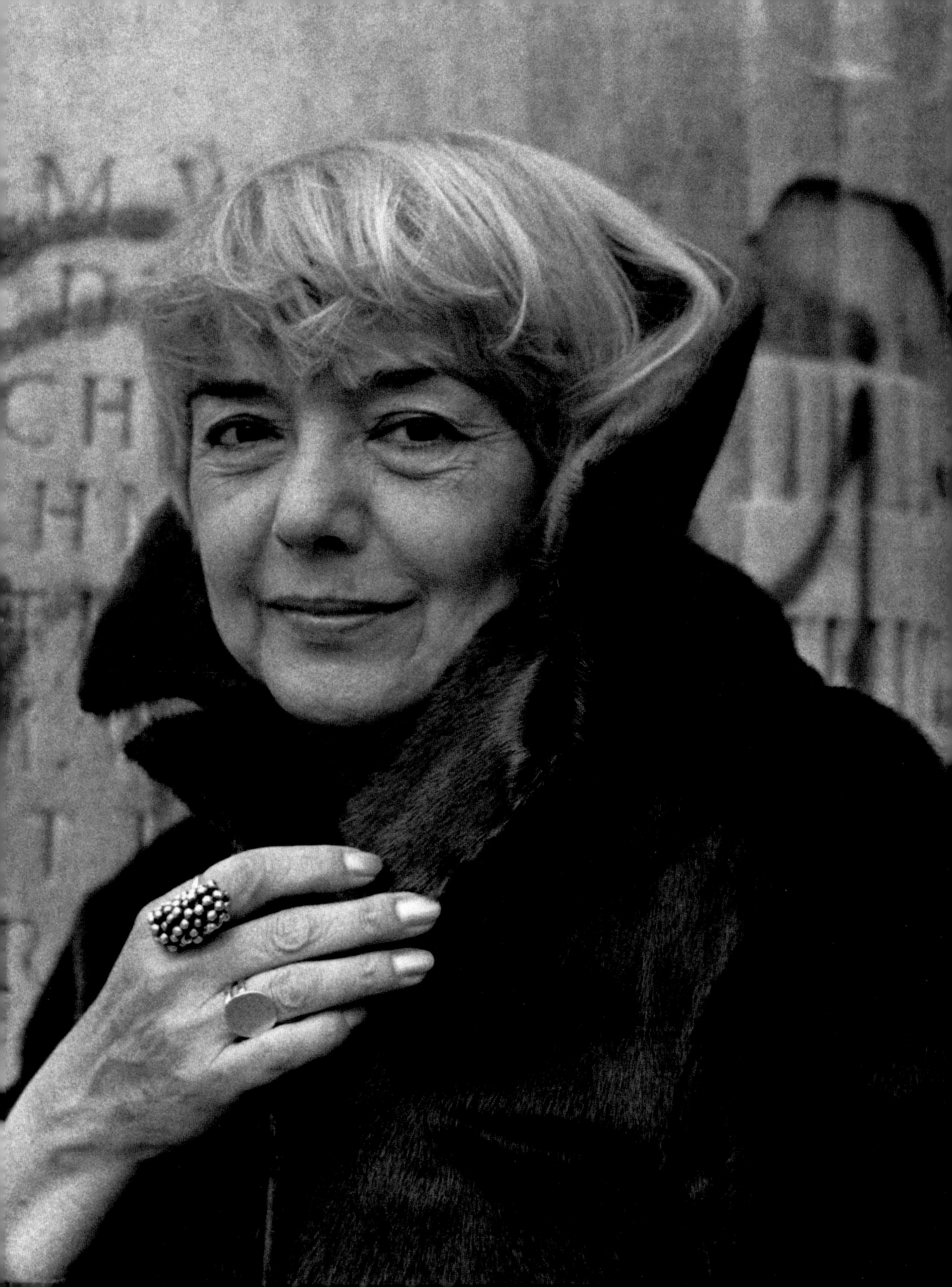

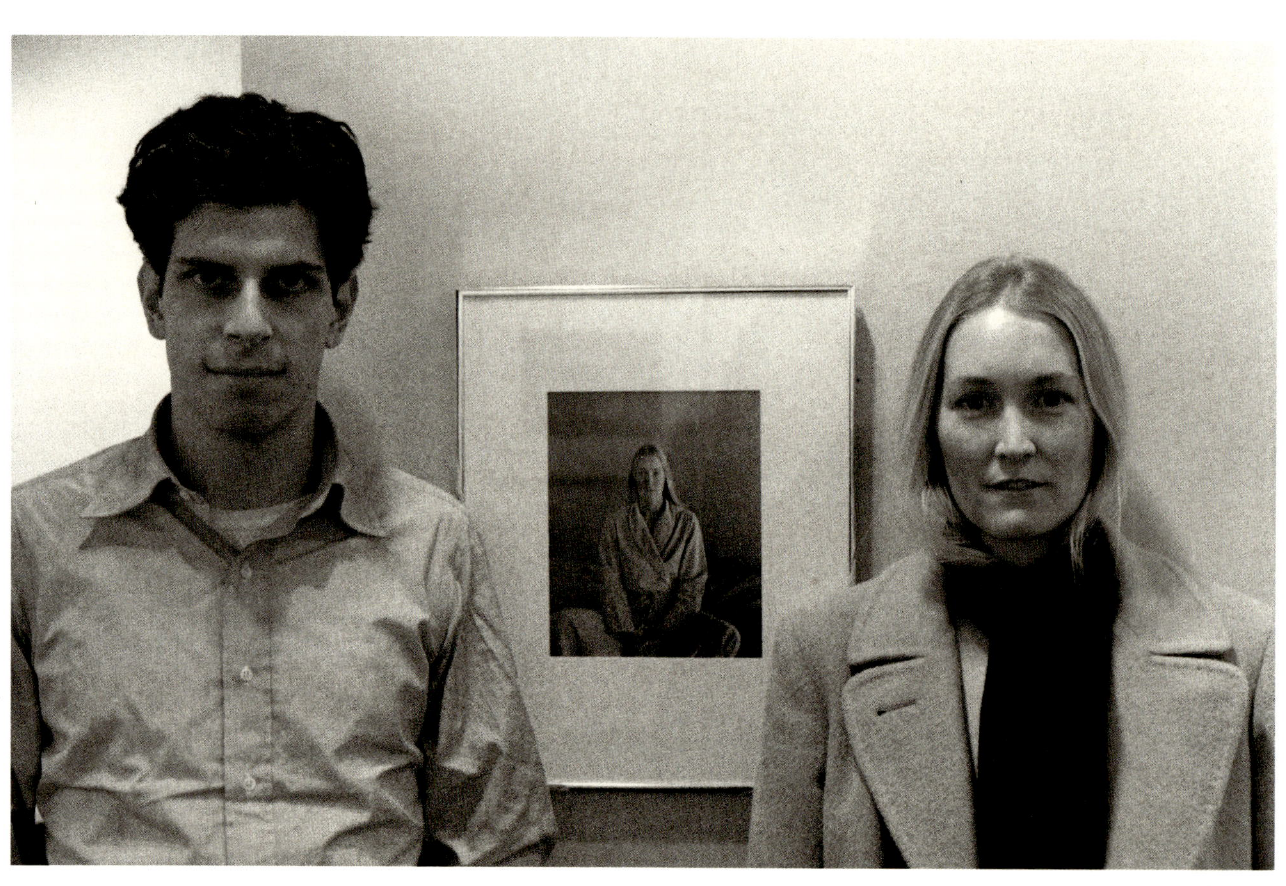

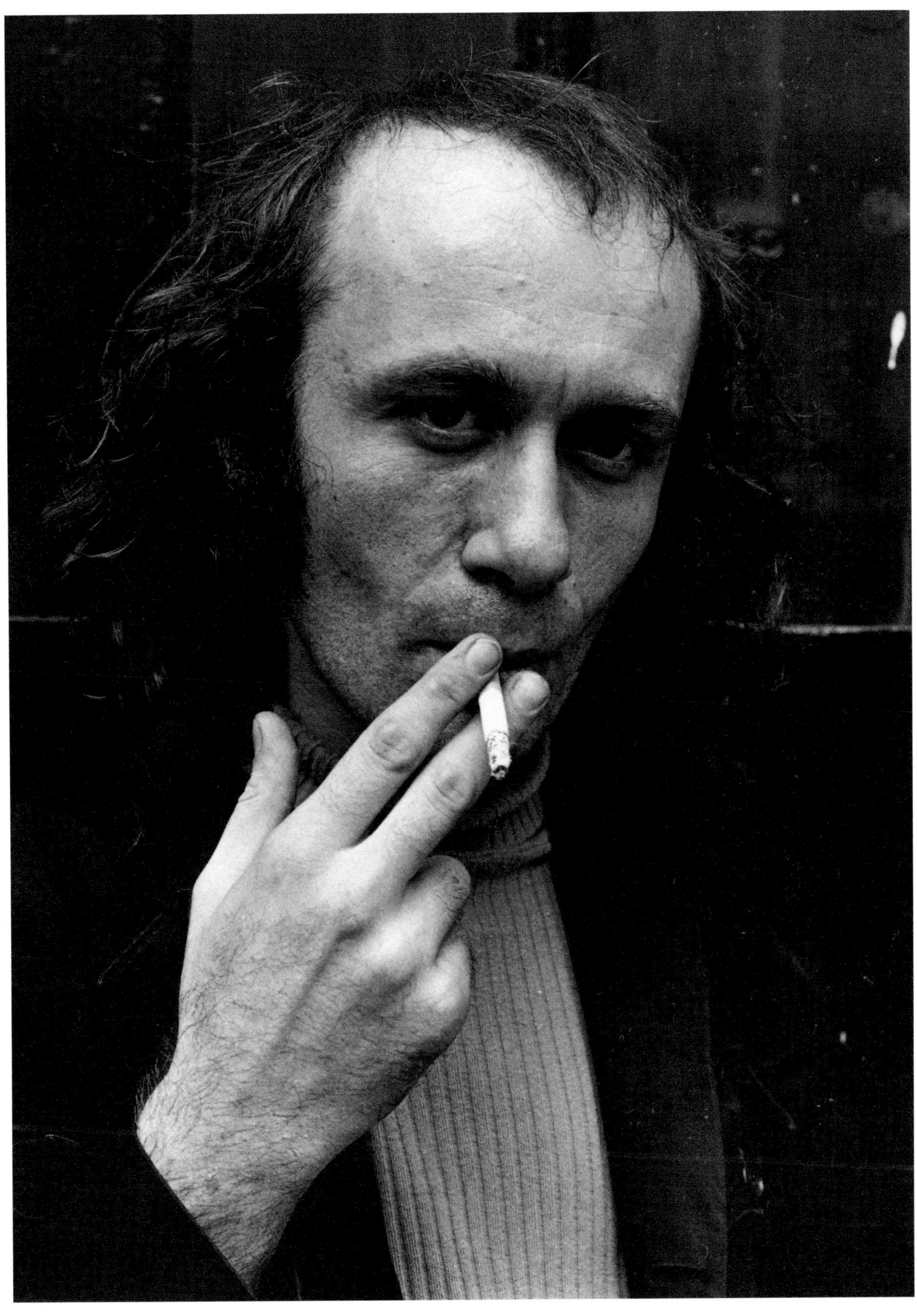

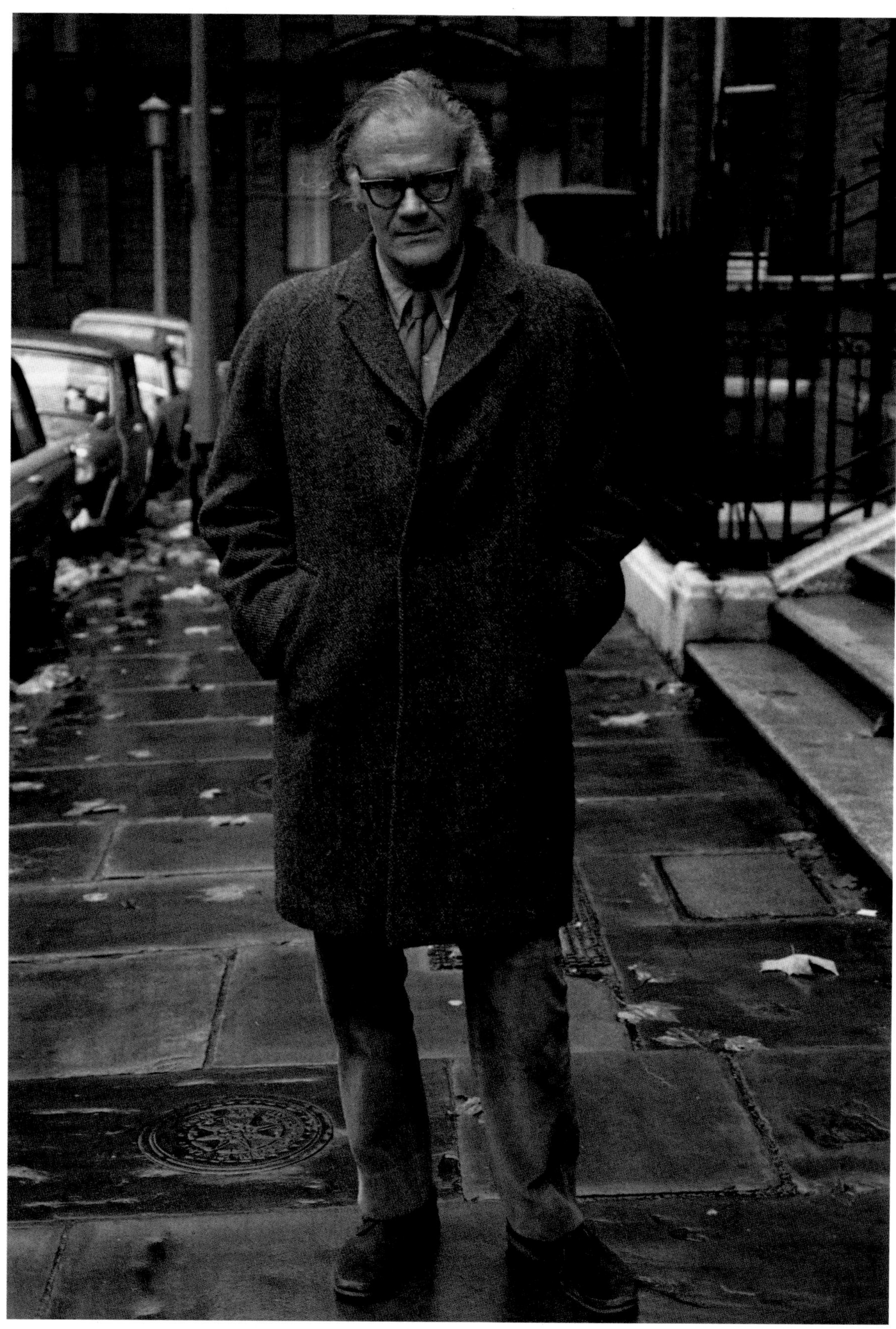

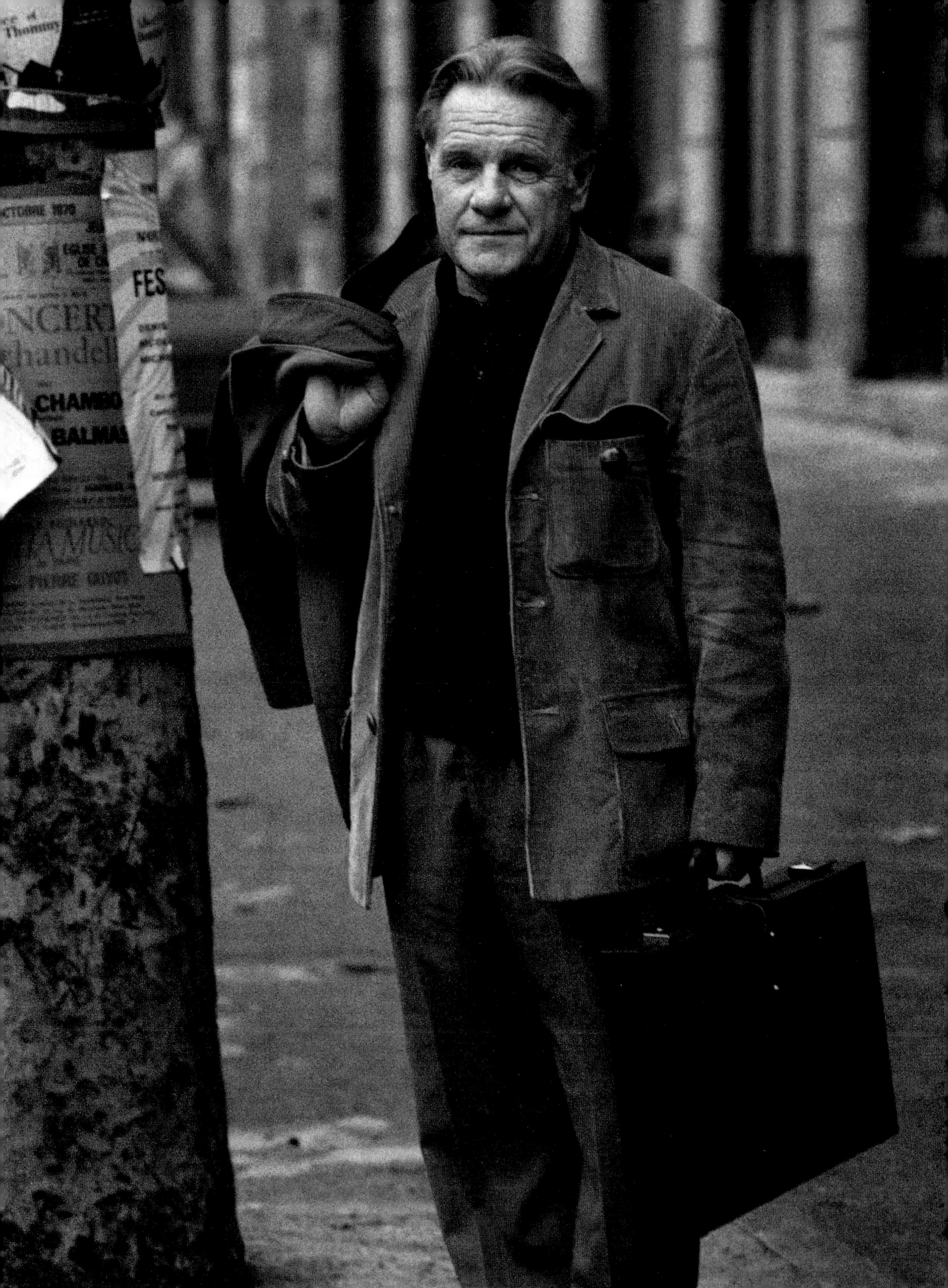

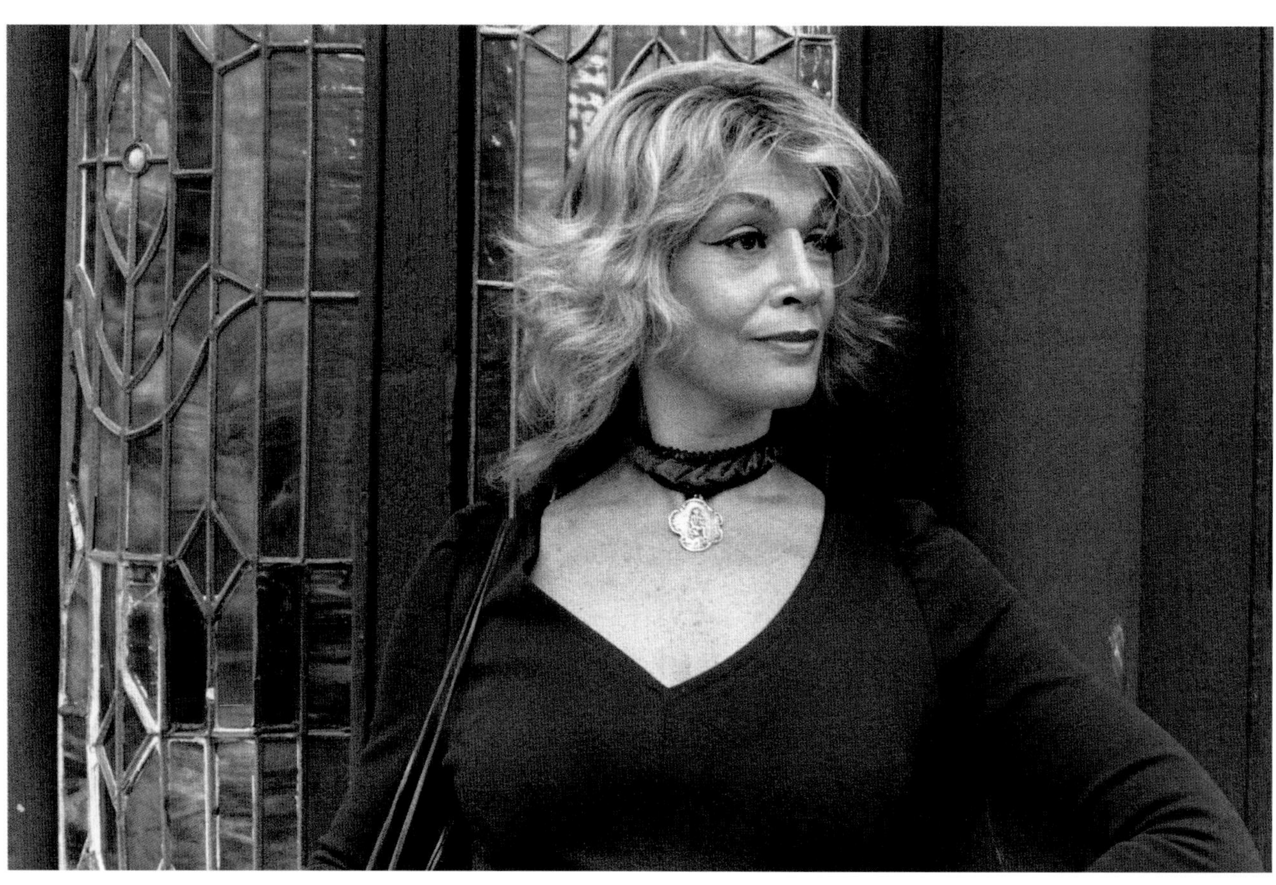

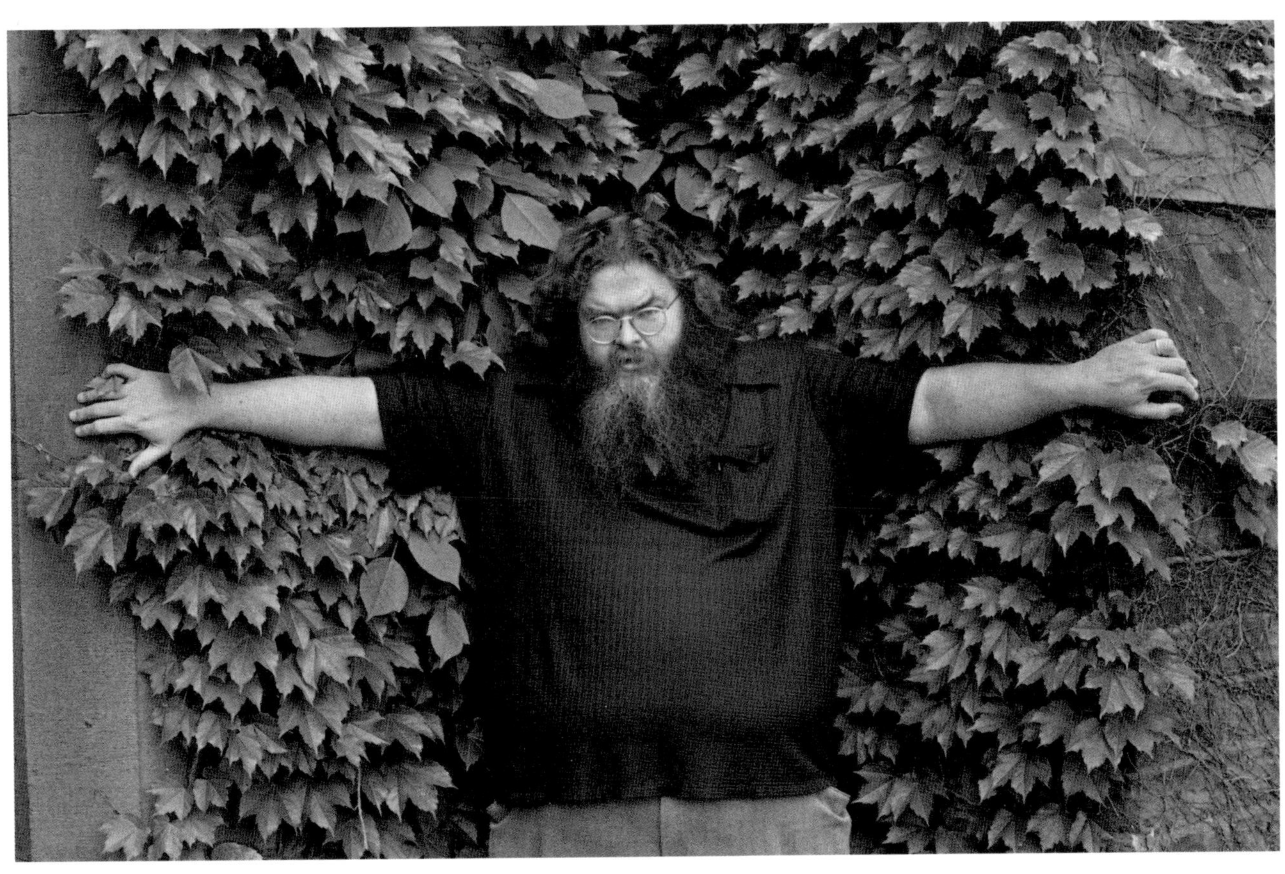

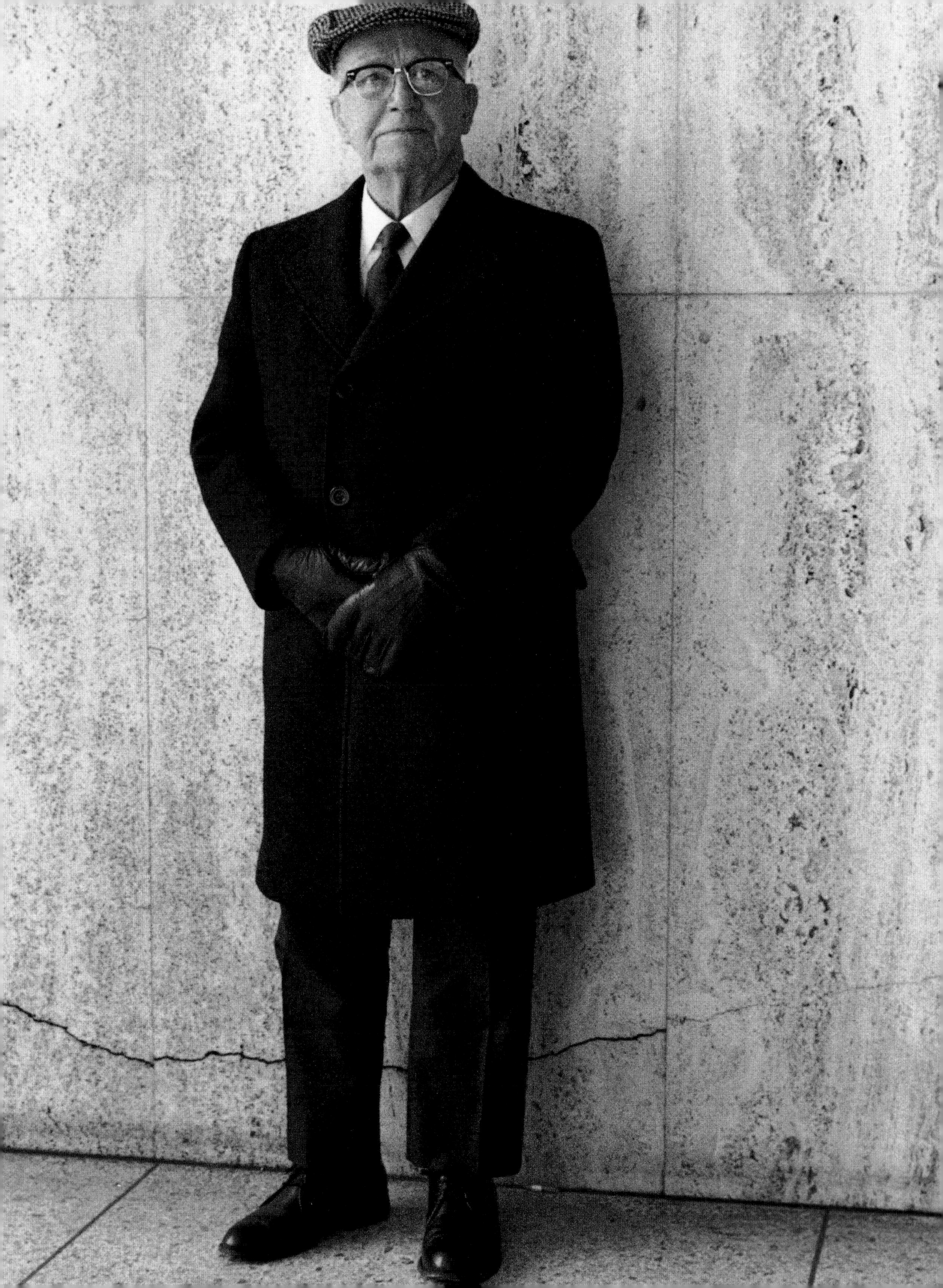

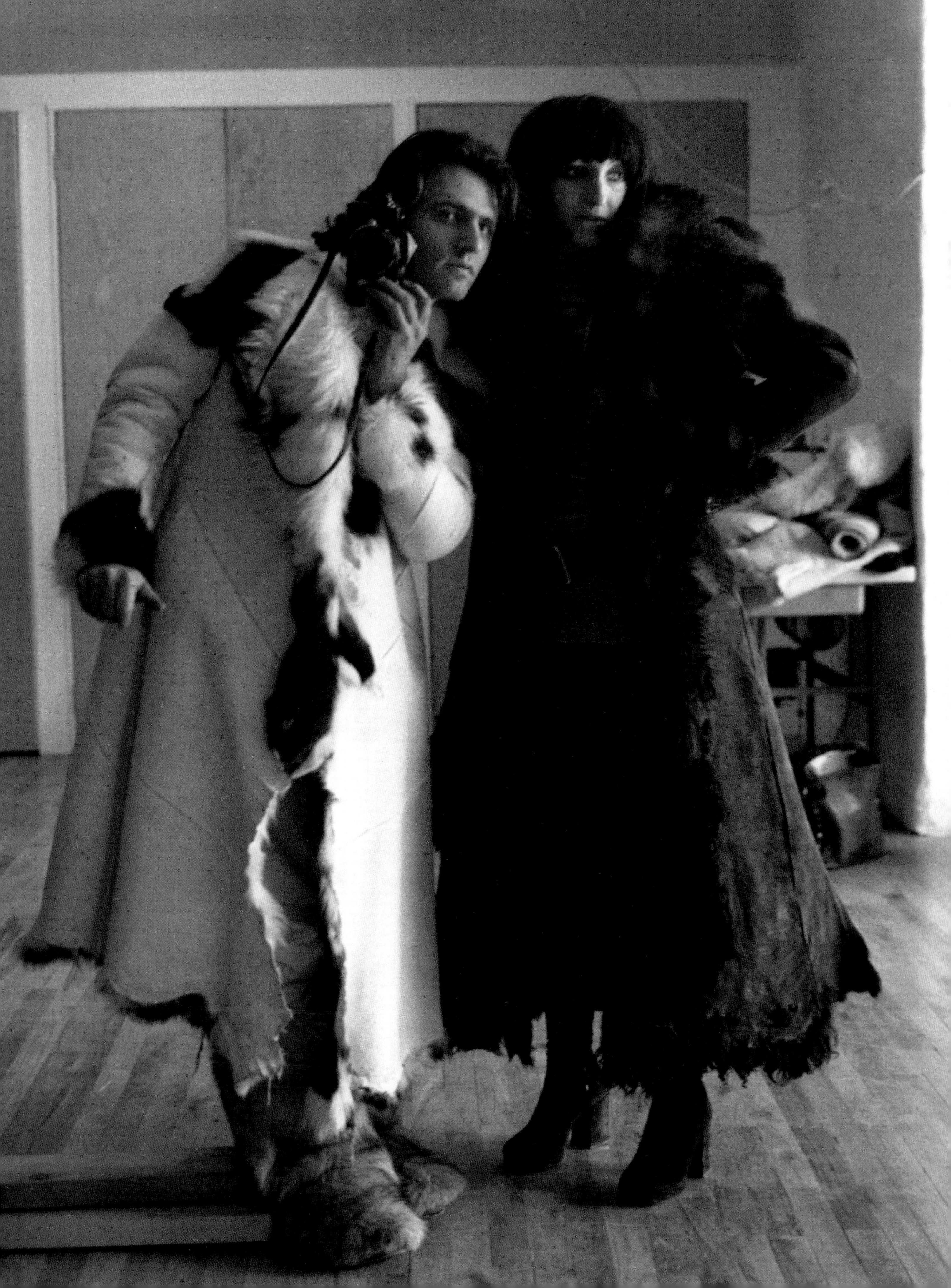

list of plates

24 *Sam Shepard & Patti Smith, London,* 1972, gelatin silver print, 14" x 11"

25 *Sam Shepard & Patti Smith as they appeared in the one night performance of their play* Cowboy Mouth, *New York City,* 1971, gelatin silver print, 11" x 14"

26 *Tennessee Williams, New York City,* 1975, gelatin silver print, 14" x 11"

27 *Christopher Isherwood, New York City,* 1976, gelatin silver print, 14" x 11"

28 *Stephen Spender,* 1976, gelatin silver print, 11" x 14"

29 *Galway Kinnell with his children, Mande & Pancho Fergus, New York City,* 1971, gelatin silver print, 14" x 11"

30 *Anne Waldman, New York City,* 1970, gelatin silver print, 14" x 11"

31 *Roman Polanski, London,* 1972, gelatin silver print, 14" x 11"

32 *Charles Henri Ford, Xania, Crete,* 1972, gelatin silver print, 11" x 14"

33 *Lotte Lenya, New York City,* 1974, gelatin silver print, 14" x 11"

34 *Leigh Taylor-Young, New York City,* 1971, gelatin silver print, 14" x 11"

35 *Iggy Pop, New York City,* 1971, gelatin silver print, 14" x 11"

36 *Cybill Shepherd, New York City,* 1971, gelatin silver print, 14" x 11"

37 *Kelly Klein, née Kelly Rector, Central Park, New York City,* 1971, gelatin silver print, 14" x 11"

38 *Zero Mostel in his studio, New York City,* 1975, gelatin silver print, 14" x 11"

39 *Ted Berrigan, East Village, New York City,* 1971, gelatin silver print, 11" x 14"

40 *Wallace Berman, Topanga Canyon, CA,* 1972, gelatin silver print, 11" x 14"

41 *John Ashbery, New York City,* 1971, gelatin silver print, 14" x 11"

42 *John Cage, New York City,* 1974, gelatin silver print, 11" x 14"

43 *David Byrne,* 1975, gelatin silver print, 14" x 11"

44 *Louis & Celia Zukofsky, Port Jefferson, New York,* 1975, gelatin silver print, 14" x 11"

45 *Jorge Luis Borges, New York City,* 1976, gelatin silver print, 14" x 11"

46 *Erté, New York City,* 1971, gelatin silver print, 14" x 11"

47 *Jasper Johns, New York City,* 1971, gelatin silver print, 14" x 11"

48 *Henry Geldzahler, New York City,* 1971, gelatin silver print, 14" x 11"

49 *Anita Pallenberg, Frankfurt, Germany,* 1970, gelatin silver print, 14" x 11"

50 *Mick Jagger, Frankfurt, Germany,* 1970, gelatin silver print, 14" x 11"

51 *Keith Richards, North Salem, NY,* 1977, gelatin silver print, 11" x 14"

52 *George Plimpton, New York City,* 1974, gelatin silver print, 11" x 14"

53 *Loulou de la Falaise, New York City,* 1971, gelatin silver print, 14" x 11"

54 *Joe Brainard,* 1971, gelatin silver print, 11" x 14"

55 *Lou Reed, Lenox, MA,* 1973, gelatin silver print, 14" x 11"

56 *Richard Eberhart, rooftop, Hotel Chelsea,* 1975, gelatin silver print, 14" x 11"

57 *Isaac Bashevis Singer,* 1974, gelatin silver print, 14" x 11"

58 *Ira Cohen, One World Poetry '79 Festival, Amsterdam,* 1979, gelatin silver print, 11" x 14"

59 *Anthony Hecht, New York City,* 1971, gelatin silver print, 14" x 11"

60 *Dr. Rollo May, Central Park, New York City,* 1975, gelatin silver print, 14" x 11"

61 *Ray Brock, Lee, MA,* 1973, gelatin silver print, 14" x 11"

62 *Louis Waldon and son, Scott, New York City,* 1976, gelatin silver print, 14" x 11"

63 *Fernanda Sotsass Pivano, New York City,* 1976, gelatin silver print, 11" x 14"

64 *Stephen Shore & Sandy Marsh with Stephen's photo-portrait of Sandy at the Light Gallery, New York City,* 1976, gelatin silver print, 11" x 14"

65 *Vito Acconci,* 1971, gelatin silver print, 14" x 11"

66 *Robert Lowell, London,* 1970, gelatin silver print, 14" x 11"

67 *Lawrence Durrell, Paris,* 1970, gelatin silver print, 14" x 11"

68 *Sylvia Miles, New York City,* 1971, gelatin silver print, 11" x 14"

69 *Robert Kelly, Bard College, Annandale-on-Hudson, NY,* 1975, gelatin silver print, 11" x 14"

70 *Buckminster Fuller, New York City,* 1976, gelatin silver print, 14" x 11"

71 *Larissa Jarzombek and Gerard Malanga, New York City,* 1972, gelatin silver print, 14" x 11"

First Edition Published by Arena Editions
243 Closson Street, Suite 12
Santa Fe, New Mexico 87501-2533, USA
505.986.9132 tel. 505.986.9138 fax
Website: http//:www.arenaed.com

Concept: James Crump

Book Design: Elsa Kendall

Distribution by D.A.P./Distributed Art Publishers
155 Sixth Avenue, Second Floor
New York, NY 10013
212.627.1999 tel 212.627.9484 fax

Printed by EBS, Verona - Italy

First Edition, 1998.

ISBN 0-9657280-6-4

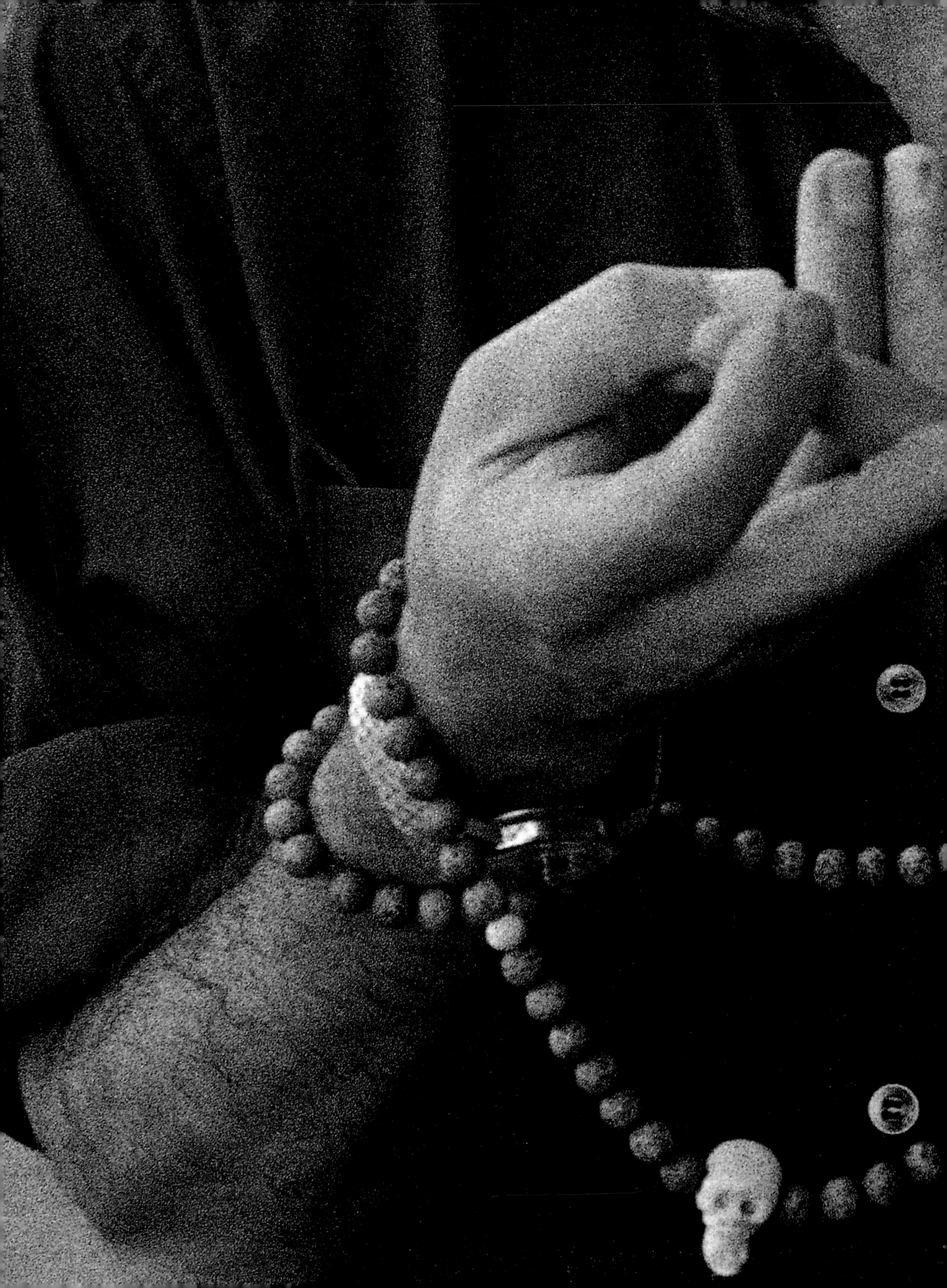